The International TENNIS GUIDE

Stan Smith, Abe Segal, Lew Hoad, and Tom Gorman after an exhibition at Lew Hoad's Campo de Tenis in Spain.

enhanced by the presence of many antiques and Bermudian artifacts.

Cambridge Beaches has two all-weather cork-turf courts. There is no tennis professional and tennis is played as a pleasant pastime only, not as a competitive sport. There is no charge for use of the courts, which are floodlit. Playing time is limited to one hour and courts can be reserved on Sundays for the whole of the following week. I have included it because it is one of the most pleasant resorts in Bermuda, both in terms of scenic beauty and the high standard of accommodations.

The hotel has two famous bonefish flats immediately adjacent to it which are big attractions for fishing enthusiasts who spend hours casting in the surf. There is also excellent shoal fishing and nearby charter boats are readily available for game fishing. As is usual in Bermuda, the beaches are superb. A championship eighteen-hole golf course at Port Royal is only a mile away and the hotel provides free transportation to it.

A disadvantage, or advantage depending on how one looks at it, of Cambridge Beaches is its remoteness from the rest of the island. Hamilton with its shops is a good half-hour drive away and the airport is another half hour beyond Hamilton. But to people seeking privacy away from crowds and commercialism, Cambridge Beaches cannot be too highly recommended.

The hotel property consists of twenty-five acres of lawns and flowering shrubs, with water on three sides. The atmosphere is congenial and informal—more like a private club than a hotel. There are fifty-five rooms, including thirty-two cottages. Rates range from $56 to $90 for double occupancy, Modified American Plan, that is, breakfast, afternoon tea, and dinner are included in the price. Prices are fifteen percent lower in the off season, from December to March.

The Castle Harbour
Tucker's Town
Bermuda

The Castle Harbour Hotel is a completely self-contained resort with its own yacht club, eighteen-hole golf course, two freshwater heated swimming pools, beaches, tennis courts, night clubs,

13

shops and restaurants. Commanding magnificent views of the Atlantic, the hotel is one of the largest in Bermuda. When it was built in the thirties it was considered to be the most modern and the most luxurious hotel in the world. Most of its former glories still remain. The two-hundred-and-thirty-acre grounds are spectacular with their beautiful flowering shrubs, rolling lawns and flower gardens. The Castle Harbour is unique in another respect—it is one of the few places in Bermuda that serves kosher food.

Although one could spend several weeks just within the hotel grounds and never be bored, Castle Harbour is well situated for exploring the island. It is close to the Crystal Caves, the Perfume Factory, Tom Moore's Tavern and the old town of St. George's. Hamilton is approximately twenty minutes away by car. A leisurely drive through Tucker's Town to see the most fabulous villas in Bermuda is a must.

There are six all-weather cork-turf tennis courts here, two of which are lighted. The tennis professional, El Smith, is a past All-Bermuda champion. He gives lessons, organizes games and arranges friendly tournaments. There is no charge for the tennis facilities to tennis groups or to people on one of the special tennis-package plans, but individuals must pay $1.50 per hour. A complete pro-shop, shower facilities and soft-drink bar complete the tennis picture. Racquet restringing is not done here, but rental equipment is available. Courts cannot be booked more than a day in advance and playing time is limited to one hour. Doubles are encouraged, but not mandatory at the height of the season when the courts are most in demand.

Castle Harbour is very popular with New Yorkers, and as New York has gone tennis mad, competition is very keen. Players of all levels are to be found here—from rank beginners to good club players.

Prices vary from $54 to $80 per day for double occupancy, Modified American Plan, but there are special packages which are cheaper, particularly in the off season.

For rates, either individual or package deals, write to Mr. James Harre.

The Coral Beach and Tennis Club
Paget
Bermuda

The Coral Beach is one of the oldest and most famous of Bermuda's resorts. It is a club in the sense that most of its permanent members are residents of Bermuda and every visitor has to be introduced by a member or former guest.

The setting of the Club is absolutely magnificent. One cannot enter through its gates without sensing the graciousness of another, more leisurely era. The long drive curves upward through lawns and trees, first past the tennis courts, then the putting green, and on to the main building. This building houses the lounge, cocktail bar, and dining room. Cedar paneling, shining wood floors, chintzes and flowers create a comfortable country-house atmosphere.

The dining area is down a few steps and one dines either inside or outdoors on a terrace overlooking the sea, depending on the weather. The food, service, and setting are considered to be even among Bermudians the best on the island. The Wednesday-night barbecues are particularly lavish and are very popular with members and guests alike.

Below all this lies a magnificent coral-sand beach, owned by the Club. More terraces with a separate bar and snack restaurant have been placed near the steps which lead down to the sea, so that one may have lunch or a drink completely informally, without entering the main building. Their chef's salad is the best I have ever tasted anywhere.

The rooms, seaside cottages, and garden cottages are tastefully furnished and are outstanding for their privacy and seclusion. The Club can accommodate a total of one hundred and thirty people.

The tennis club has six clay and one dynaturf court, a pro-shop, bar, terrace and showers. The pro is Derek Singleton, who, together with a charming English woman, Sheena Lamb, handles lessons, bookings, and runs the pro-shop. The charge for one court per hour is $4.75 for non-members. Members pay a $.75 reservation fee only. Court reservations may be made only two

The Coral Beach and Tennis Club in Bermuda has six excellent clay courts in an idyllic sub-tropical setting.

days in advance. Two courts are lighted for night play. As this is *the* tennis spot in Bermuda, the caliber of play is high. Sunday afternoon mixed-doubles round robins are very popular with members and guests.

Unlike many other tennis resorts, singles can be played at any time, even at peak periods. Because of the fairly steep price of courts, finding people to play with is very easy—if you book the court. Restringing is done here, also rental racquets are available. A half-hour lesson costs $9.00. There are tennis clinics for children of members and group lessons for adults which cost $2.00 per person. There are no teaching aids such as ball or video-tape machines. January and February are the quietest months; at other times you must hustle to get enough court time.

The Coral Beach Invitation Tournament is held here every November and is officially recognized by the U.S. Lawn Tennis Association for ranking purposes. This is a big sporting and social event, and tennis afficionados come from far and wide to see the tennis and to take part in all the social activities, which are held during this week.

Tennis, the beach and the putting green are the only diversions here but the Club is so well liked that even avid golfers come to stay. Located roughly in the center of the island, it is close to just about everything, but once inside the gates peace and tranquility reign.

Rates range from approximately $30 to $50 per day per person, Modified American Plan. For more information, write to the Manager.

Elbow Beach Surf Club
Paget
Bermuda

A unique feature of the Elbow Beach Surf Club is that it is built next to perhaps the most beautiful and perfect beach in the world. Wide, pink, and clean, with the turquoise water of the Atlantic lapping at its edge, this is truly an almost perfect beach. The hotel runs a restaurant-terrace-souvenir shop complex next to the beach which is a convenience, but rather an eyesore.

Four all-weather tennis courts and a tennis professional are available to guests at The Holiday Inn in Bermuda.

The Elbow Beach is a big hotel of approximately five-hundred rooms, offering all the activities and amenities of a large hotel—shops, a night club, heated swimming pool, games room, snack bar, shuffleboard court, bar, live entertainment, local bands and a good dining room.

There are two all-weather tennis courts, but no professional. Courts are only for the use of the guests with the Sunday round robin being the tennis highlight of the week. The social hostess will arrange games. The courts do not have lights, but there is a charge of $1.00 per hour for their use. There is a small pro-shop with some very attractive Fred Perry tennis clothing for sale at reasonable prices. Tennis is not really organized here, but is played on a first come, first served basis.

Located conveniently close to Hamilton, the Elbow Beach offers a variety of accommodations—cottages, terraced bedrooms, lanai suites and sea-garden suites. There is no golf course on the property, but golf is never far away in Bermuda. A medium-price hotel, the Elbow Beach is popular with honeymooners and singles, although the winter draws a slightly older crowd. For more information on rates, package tours and honeymoon specials, write to the Reservations Manager.

Holiday Inn

P.O. Box 59
St. George's
Bermuda

The Bermuda Holiday Inn, perched on a hillside overlooking the Atlantic, is the only hotel in the historic town of St. George's. St. George's boasts of being the oldest settlement in North America and presents a fascinating bird's eye view of the past. Many of the old buildings have been carefully restored and are open for inspection. It is located on the easternmost tip of the island, which means that it is very close to the airport, but some distance away from Hamilton and other points of interest. However, as Bermuda is only twenty-one miles long, this is not a great drawback.

The Holiday Inn has 297 rooms, forty-one suites, two heated fresh-water swimming pools, a nine hole golf course, water skiing, sailing, deep-sea and reef fishing. Evening entertainment is also plentiful. The Mid-Atlantic Supper Club features both local and international acts. Pierre's Nightclub, The Sea Venture Bar for dancing, and Strachy's Watch, a bar on the tenth floor with a marvellous view of Bermuda, are the other pleasure domes. Every room has a radio, television, air conditioner, telephone and bathroom. By and large, they are well and tastefully furnished.

The Inn has four all-weather tennis courts. The tennis professional, Donald Lottimore, is actively involved with both private lessons and clinics. Private lessons are $8.00 per half hour. Group lessons are a bargain at $3.00 per hour. He also does his best to arrange games. All the courts are lighted for night play. A complete pro-shop with restringing facilities and showers completes the tennis picture. Tennis is a very popular sport at the Holiday Inn, both among the guests and residents of the area, who may become members of a special tennis section. There is a charge of $2.00 per hour per court. Friendly tournaments and round robins are held whenever there is a demand for them. The Holiday Inn is fast becoming one of Bermuda's top tennis centers.

This hotel is for people who like the liveliness of a big hotel with its attendant variety of faces, activities and services. You will get good value for your money here. In Bermuda nothing is cheap, but the Holiday Inn offers some good package deals. To find out about special group rates, honeymoon plans, and other packages write to Mr. J. B. Smith, General Manager.

Pink Beach Cottage Colony

Tucker's Town
Bermuda

Although not primarily a tennis resort, the Pink Beach Cottage Colony has been included because it is such a pleasant place to stay and it does have two tennis courts.

Located in a very exclusive section of Bermuda on a lovely

stretch of beach, Pink Beach is a collection of fifty pink cottages and one main house. Having only accommodation for a hundred people, guests at the Pink Beach get to know one another quickly.

There are two California-type hard courts here, no professional, and there is no charge for use of the courts. Even though tennis is not organized in any way, there is keen competition among the tennis-playing guests and finding a game is never a problem. Playing time is unlimited. There are no lights. Both the courts and the heated swimming pool are used all the year around.

An outstanding feature of Pink Beach is the excellence of its food. The management is lavish with luxury items, the chef is imaginative, and the service is fast, and efficient.

Rates vary from $64 to $110 for double occupancy, Modified American Plan. Prices are approximately fifteen percent lower in the off season, December to March. This charming cottage colony is one of the top three resort hotels on the island, and those who can afford the rather stiff prices are assured a happy holiday.

If you can tear yourself away from the fabulous hotel dinners, Tom Moore's Tavern is a good place to go. Dinners here are even better than the lunches, and the servings are enormous. The Bermuda fish chowder should not be missed. Overrun by tourists during the lunch hours, Tom Moore's Tavern is popular with native Bermudians for dinner.

Pomander Gate Club and Cottages

Paget
Bermuda

Pleasantly situated on a narrow, winding road close to Hamilton, the Pomander Gate Club was originally a small guest house, renowned for its hospitality and excellent home cooking. Although expanded and modernized, it has retained much of its original charm, and at the same time now has all the latest modern conveniences.

Consisting of twenty-five rooms and four cottages, the Pomander Gate Club rates vary between $22 to $26 per person per day, including breakfast, dinner and afternoon tea. There is a swimming pool and a private beach club on the premises.

Tennis is the big sport at Pomander Gate. There are four all-weather, laykold tennis courts here, two teaching professionals and a good standard of tennis all the year around. There is no charge for use of the courts. The professional, Cromwell Manders gives adults private lessons only, but there are special clinics for children. A half-hour lesson costs $12. Racquet restringing is not done on the premises. Courts have to be reserved a day ahead, and getting enough court time can be a problem. January and February are the slackest months, but then the weather may let you down.

The Pomander Gate Club, besides catering to hotel guests, is also a private Bermudian tennis club with a young and very active membership. Hotel guests are mainly young people from the Eastern Seaboard and Canada. Every Wednesday afternoon there is a ladies round robin and tea, to which hotel guests are invited. A mixed-doubles round robin is held every Saturday afternoon, also with the inevitable tea.

Tennis, the beach and the pool are the main diversions here. If you wish to golf, sail, water ski or fish, the front desk will be very happy to arrange it for you. For shopping, Hamilton is only a five-minute ferry ride away.

Southampton Princess Hotel

Southampton
Bermuda

The Southampton Princess looms like a transplanted Miami Beach hotel on the conservative Bermuda landscape. It is the largest hotel on the island—three hundred more rooms have recently been added—and it has all the side attractions that make up the large hotel: nightclubs, cabarets, bars, restaurants, shopping plazas, and a vast mezzanine.

However, the beach and the beach club are spectacular, with one of the most beautiful white-coral beaches to be found anywhere. A free shuttle service runs between the beach club and the hotel. It is within the beach-club complex that six of the eleven tennis courts are to be found. Two are lighted for night play. Bob Alger, the professional, gives private lessons only, at $10 per half hour. There is a charge of $3.00 an hour per court. The social hostess arranges games when desired. Round robins are staged whenever there is a demand for them, mostly during the winter months. Getting enough court time is not a problem here yet, but with the number of tennis players constantly increasing, it may soon become one. There is a complete pro-shop with showers, bar and a wide range of tennis fashions and equipment. Racquet restringing is done on the premises. The other five courts are very new and are located next to the hotel.

There is a beautiful eighteen-hole golf course surrounding the hotel. The clientele consists mainly of well-heeled Americans and Canadians of indeterminate age, plus the odd honeymoon couple who can afford the Princess's stiff prices.

Although water sports, sightseeing and shopping trips are popular activities, tennis, golf and gourmandizing are the main preoccupations of the guests. The hotel is open all the year around and is particularly popular with golfers during the winter months.

Rates vary from $40 to $200 (for the penthouse) per day, Modified American Plan. For more information, write to the Reservations Manager.

The Inn on the Park's laykold all-weather courts in Toronto are equipped for both daytime and night play.

CHAPTER 2
CANADA

Although Canadian nationalists do not like to hear it, there are relatively few cultural and sociological differences between the United States and Canada. The exception, of course, is the Province of Quebec, which is a completely different experience. Montreal has a style of its own; it has a slightly schizophrenic personality due to its two ethnic groups who have spent a long time trying to overpower, assimilate and emulate each other. It is a beautiful city with its situation as an island mountain. It boasts a wonderful selection of fine French restaurants, some of which are in the picturesque old quarter. It also has a very lively night life. There are many high-quality boutiques and some very good department stores.

Quebec City should not be by-passed. It is the only walled city in North America. The best way to see it is to take a walking tour through its narrow winding streets starting from the upper town down through the lower town. The Plains of Abraham offer a spectacular view of the St. Lawrence River. Instead of shopping in Quebec City, which doesn't offer much variety, one's time is far better spent enjoying the French habit of superb lengthy meals.

To enter Canada, all you need is proof of identification. The Canadian dollar is worth approximately the same as the American dollar and is freely accepted everywhere.

Banff Springs Hotel

Banff
Alberta

The Banff Springs Hotel is a large, baronial castle which stands at the junction of the Bow and Spray Rivers, amid a circle of majestic mountains in the huge wilderness area known as Banff National Park.

The village of Banff has recently seen an upsurge of interest in the performing arts and it is now a lively place with summer theaters, restaurants, handicraft boutiques and music and arts camps. For outdoor sports it is, of course, magnificent. The fresh mountain air and beautiful scenery act as powerful magnets in drawing everyone outdoors. Situated at an altitude of 4,625 feet, summer temperatures range from mild to brisk.

The Banff Springs Hotel golf course is one of the world's most beautiful championship courses, eighteen holes, 6,704 yards, par 71. The Club House and first tee are only a hundred yards from the hotel. A fully equipped pro-shop is in the Club House. Caddies and motorized carts are available.

There is good fishing in many of the nearby mountain lakes and streams of Banff National Park. Dolly Varden, grayling, rainbow, cutthroat and Nipigon trout offer thrilling sport. An experienced fishing advisor is at the hotel to arrange fishing parties and to give advice as to where the best fishing spots are.

Swimming in the heated pool, shuffleboard, mountain climbing and tennis are the other sports activities. Tennis is played on five all-weather courts. A pro is available to give lessons and to arrange games. The courts do not have lights. There is a small pro-shop where rental equipment is available, but it has no restringing facilities. The season lasts only from June to the end of September, but tennis interest is on the rise and many friendly round robins are played throughout the summer. Finding a congenial game is not hard, particularly if you spend time in the court area and make an effort to meet the people who play your game. There is no charge for hotel guests and courts do not have to be reserved. Getting enough court time is not a problem.

Trail riding through the many beautiful mountain trails; excursions to Lake Louise; the Victoria Glacier, where it sometimes snows in mid-summer; The Lakes in the Clouds; Stoney Indian Reserve; Radium Hot Springs; the Columbia Ice Fields; all of these are enjoyable activities and outings.

Americans and Canadians come to Banff in almost equal numbers. This is primarily a family hotel and many satisfied clients return year after year. The hotel operates on European

Plan with prices ranging from $28 to $32 for a double room. Special convention and group rates are available. Banff is accessible by car (it is on the Trans-Canada Highway between Calgary and Vancouver), by train, or by plane. The nearest airport is in Calgary, forty miles away.

Clevelands House

Minnett
Ontario
Canada

Clevelands House, established in 1869, is one of the more charming of the inns that dot the picturesque Muskoka Lake area. It is practically a historic site, now modernized, famous for its informality, good hearty food and a typically friendly Canadian atmosphere. When you first arrive you will be struck by the freshness of the air, the smell of the pine woods, and the clear crisp cleanliness of this very special part of Canada.

A wide range of activities are provided for hotel guests. Swimming in Lake Rousseau, or in the eighty-foot heated pool, golfing on a nine-hole golf course, water skiing under the guidance of a professional, horseback riding and hiking on secluded sugarbush trails, and fishing for smallmouth bass or lake trout are all favorite activities.

Tennis is an important sport at Clevelands House. There are two en-tous-cas courts and three all-weather courts, rated among the best in Canada. A professional is on hand to give lessons and arrange games. There are weekly guest tournaments, as well as the Muskoka Lakes Championships in July, which attract high-caliber tennis players. There is no charge for court time for hotel guests and playing time is unlimited. You do not have to reserve, but you may find yourself waiting in line. A small pro-shop is on the premises, but it does not do restringing.

The hotel can accommodate approximately three-hundred people and it is an ideal family hotel. They are used to children here and try very hard to amuse and look after them. Planned children's programs, special dining-room sittings, a nursery and

Gray Rocks Inn, in St. Jovite, Quebec has four fast-drying rubico tennis courts and a complete tennis program for guests.

a bountiful supply of baby sitters, all help to make parents' holidays very pleasant.

Rates start around $21 per person per day, full American Plan and go up to $31 per day depending on the quality of the room. There are many special packages. The hotel is open from mid-May until October. It is approximately 139 miles from Toronto and the easiest way to get there is to drive. Alternately, there is a rail service to Mactier, nineteen miles away. Clevelands House is by far the most active tennis spot of the Muskoka area. For more information write to Mr. Robert E. Cornell, Manager.

Gray Rocks Inn

St. Jovite
Province of Quebec
Canada

Both Americans and Canadians flock to Quebec because it is so different from the rest of North America. In Quebec there is always time to enjoy a well-cooked meal, to laugh with friends, and to have a good time.

Gray Rocks Inn is no exception to these French Canadian traditions. A conglomerate of three buildings—the Lodge itself, the de luxe Chalet Suisse, and Le Chateau, a swinging singles' spot located a short distance away with its own dining room and swimming pool, Gray Rocks is situated on the shores of Lac Ouimet, approximately seventy-four miles north of Montreal.

Tennis is offered to guests of the hotel at no charge. There are four fast-drying rubico courts, playable between May 1 and November 10. Private lessons are available at $4 for half an hour and $7 for one hour. There is a complete pro-shop on the premises with rental equipment and restringing facilities. Gray Rocks has a unique tennis program to lure tennis-playing guests. This is an all-inclusive price for seven days and seven nights, covering room, meals, and five one-hour lessons. Instruction includes sessions on strategy, use of audio-visual aids and presentation of tennis films. There are also weekly tournaments with awards. The cost for this tennis package, with room and private bath ranges from $137.50 to $183.50; without bath, but with running water from $110 to $120. Gray Rocks is not the place for the tennis addict; generally speaking the caliber of tennis is not very high. Rather, it is geared for the novice and intermediate player who wants to improve his game and have a good time. All the water sports are here, as well as eighteen holes of golf, riding, volleyball, shuffleboard, lawn bowling and a putting green.

The Inn goes out of its way to entertain and monitor children, consequently parents can have a great deal of freedom, if they want it. There is a 4700-foot air strip half a mile from the Inn for people who fly their own planes. Live entertainment, dances, and other social activities are arranged by the social hostess. Dress is very informal, although a jacket and tie are required for dinner.

Inn On The Park

1100 Eglinton Avenue East
Don Mills, Toronto
Ontario M3C 1H8
Canada

The Inn on the Park, Toronto's luxury resort and convention hotel, has three lighted, hard-surface (laykold) tennis courts, two of which are lighted for night-play from October to June. From June 1 to October 1 all courts operate from dawn to dusk. Two of the courts are indoor and are open all the year around. The third court is open air, and is in operation from June to October.

Reservations for courts are accepted the whole year around. From October 1 to June 1 fees for use of courts are $8 per hour before 4 p.m. on weekdays; and $10 per hour after 4 p.m., Saturdays, Sundays and holidays. From June 1 to October 1 no fee is charged to hotel guests for use of the tennis courts.

There is a charge of $6 for one hour of instruction (plus court fee) in the winter months; $10 is charged for a one-hour lesson in the summer (when there is no court fee). Douglas Owen-Hicks is the tennis professional. Throughout the year, Mr.

Owen-Hicks conducts a special Saturday morning tennis clinic for hotel guests between 9 a.m. and 11 a.m. and the charge per guest is $5 for a two-hour session. Guests wishing to rent or to buy tennis equipment can do so through the pro-shop at the Inn.

The tennis players here are usually businessmen passing through Toronto who want to play tennis in their free time. Games are easily arranged through the pro-shop. There is also an active local membership during the winter months.

Other sports facilities at the Inn on the Park include The Health Club with wet and dry saunas; indoor or outdoor jogging tracks; indoor and outdoor swimming pools; a whirlpool bath; and games such as shuffleboard, badminton and table tennis.

The hotel has 609 rooms, with prices ranging from $31 to $38 (double occupancy, European Plan). Special weekend packages ($69.50 for two) are offered from September to June. Four good restaurants and three lounges offer a variety of entertainment. Parking for one thousand cars is free. The Inn on the Park is surrounded by parkland, fifteen minutes from downtown Toronto and five minutes from the Ontario Science Center.

Jasper Park Lodge

Jasper
Alberta

Located about a two-and-a-half-hour drive from Calgary through some of the world's most awesome scenery, Jasper Park Lodge is a little village of cedar chalets nestled among pines and spread out along an unspoiled mountain lake. Avid fishermen get up early and catch a couple of trout for breakfast. A hundred-and-sixty-room hotel, Jasper Park Lodge is an outdoorsman's paradise. Great fishing, mountain climbing, riding through miles of private trails, golf on an eighteen-hole championship course where every hole is lined up with a mountain peak, swimming either in the heated pool or in numerous mountain lakes — all these activities can be enjoyed amid the grandeur of mountains, gorges and waterfalls.

The food is good, standard hotel fare. Culinary highlights are steaks, for which Alberta is justly famous. Movies, dinner dancing, cards and table tennis are the evening activities.

There are four excellent clay tennis courts situated next to the main building. The courts are always kept in first-class condition and tennis is a popular sport among the younger guests. Courts have to be reserved, but this can be done on the same day. A pro is in attendance from the beginning of June until the end of September. Tennis clinics for children are held during July and August. A small pro-shop is located in the main building with rental tennis racquets, should yours break. There is no charge for use of the courts, which are not lighted.

Jasper Park Lodge operates on European Plan (no meals included). The price of a double room varies from $10 to $12 per day per person. The lodge is a popular convention center in June and September. During July and August it is primarily a family hotel and special family plans are available. Consult your travel agent for reservations or further information.

Manoir Richelieu

Murray Bay
Pointe-au-Pic
Quebec, Canada

Your trip to Manoir Richelieu can take you through two of North America's most fascinating cities — Montreal and Quebec City. The ninety-mile drive from Quebec City to the hotel is one of the most scenically beautiful on the continent.

An enormous Gothic building dating from a grander era, the Manoir Richelieu has long been recognized as one of Canada's best resort hotels. Now modernized and under new management, the same people still come back summer after summer, mainly because of the beauty of the setting, the excellence of the food, and the wide variety of sports activities. Carved out of the forest, the Manoir is set on a green mountain-side, facing south over the fifteen-mile-wide St. Lawrence River. The air is free of ragweed, the temperatures range from brisk to perfect, and the smell of the ever-present forest is heady perfume to jaded city dwellers.

The dining room, although cavernous, has an excellent French cuisine, with many French Canadian delicacies. In general, Quebec has the highest standard of food on the North American continent and the Manoir Richelieu exemplifies this tradition.

Besides golf on a championship eighteen-hole course, there is swimming in an olympic-size pool, trap and skeet shooting, putting (eighteen holes), croquet, lawn bowling, riding and superb fly fishing in nearby lakes and rivers. Indoors, there are facilities for badminton, billiards, table tennis and bridge.

The hotel operates three en-tous-cas tennnis courts. The season runs from late May to mid October only. The sports department is headed by a Sports Director, Edgar D. McKean III, who is in charge of all sports programs except golf. He arranges tennis matches, organizes round robins annd gets tennis players together. The tennis professional, Gilles Pepin, is fully qualified and gives lessons at reasonable rates. The assistant pro, Darrell Abbott, handles the children's program and clinics. There is a charge of $2.00 per court per hour. Tennis is a very popular sport at the Manoir Richelieu and good club players are the rule rather than the exception. The August tournament is the highlight of the tennis season. Getting enough court time is becoming an ever-increasing problem. To cope with the demand, the Hotel plans to build two additional courts in the near future.

Rates, full American Plan, range from $28 to $32 daily per person for a mountain-side room and from $34 to $35 for a river-view room. Family-style cottages dot the vast grounds; rates for these vary according to unit and plan.

Mont Tremblant Lodge
Mont Tremblant
Province of Quebec
Canada

Famous as a ski resort during the winter months, the Lodge is also open in the summer and offers to the vacationing tennis

The Mont Tremblant Lodge, with its six har-tru tennis courts, in Canada's Laurentian Mountains, offers complete tennis clinics for both adults and children.

player a very pleasant holiday at reasonable prices. Located on the shores of Lac Tremblant (ten miles long) in a magnificent mountain setting, this is a very Canadian resort, enhanced by French cooking and French conviviality.

The Lodge grounds comprise four-thousand acres of lakes and mountains. The climate from May to October usually is ideal for the activities offered here — golf on a nine-hole course with magnificent views of the Laurentians; swimming in the lake or in the heated swimming pool; fishing in Lac Tremblant, or, for the Izaak Walton, plane expeditions to the northern lake country. Water skiing and sailing are also in demand. And, of course, there is tennis.

Tennis is well organized here. The Lodge has six har-tru tennis courts lighted for night play. There is a complete pro-shop with restringing facilities and rental equipment. Group and children's clinics are held regularly. Court reservations have to be made, but there is no charge for their use. The pro, Harry Easterbrook gives private lessons at very reasonable rates — $7.00 for half an hour. After tennis, The Bath and Tennis Club is ideal for a leisurely lunch and a discussion of the finer points of one's game.

There are three types of accommodations — the Inn, the Lodge, or cottages sprinkled around the property. Rates range from $15 to $24 per person per day, American Plan, or $91 to $133 per person per week, Modified American Plan, (breakfast and dinner). These are reduced summer rates. A holiday at the Mont Tremblant Lodge is one of the few vacation bargains left.

The surrounding area is dotted with little French restaurants, antique and handicraft shops and children's amusements. The Laurentians are famous for their winter skiing, but they are equally beautiful in the summer, when the Quebecois expression "hospitality is spoken here" is particularly apt.

For more information write to the Manager.

35

The Montagu Beach Hotel in Nassau has four Teniko surfaced courts in first-class condition.

CHAPTER 3
THE CARIBBEAN

Since the advent of jet travel, the Caribbean has become an oasis of sun and warmth for the winter weary of the United States, Canada, and to a lesser degree Europe. Recently there has been a movement to promote the Caribbean as an all-year vacation paradise. Hotel prices are much cheaper in the summer, sometimes nearly by half. Of course there are good reasons for this — temperatures and humidity soar, hurricanes threaten and there is more rain. If you are willing to brave the elements, then a summer Caribbean vacation is a bargain. The clientele at that time of year in the big hotels is younger, less affluent and more fun loving.

One goes to the islands for the sun, the beaches and the sports facilities — golf, tennis, fishing, snorkeling, and sailing. Sightseeing, cultural activities, and spectator sports are of minimal interest.

As a rule, hotel food can be described as good, international fare; adequate but not exciting. Exceptions are the French West Indies where a good French cuisine prevails. Generally hotel restaurants in Puerto Rico are above average, offering some exciting spicy Spanish dishes.

With the exception of native-made crafts and clothes, duty-free shopping offers the best bargains. Unfortunately native goods are often of poor quality and workmanship.

During the day, dress at all resorts is very informal. For dinner, a jacket and tie are generally worn.

The calypso is everywhere — one even sees workers in the fields swaying to its rhythm.

The people of the islands are not as friendly as they were — even five years ago. Racial tensions do exist particularly in Jamaica and the Barbados and one must be careful not to give offense. An exception to this is Puerto Rico where an atmosphere of great friendliness and hospitality prevails.

Night life is mainly within the hotels and the larger the hotel the more active the night life. However, every town has its native nightclubs with steel bands, limbo dancers, calypso singers and other more unorthodox acts.

Official identification and a return ticket are required at all ports of entry with the exception of the United States islands for American visitors. It is advisable to have a passport — it eliminates a lot of red tape.

The Jamaican dollar equals $1.30 U.S., the Bahamian dollar is at a par with the U.S. dollar, Puerto Rico uses the U.S. dollar and Barbados has the Eastern Caribbean dollar which is worth about 54 cents U.S. Everywhere you go, you will be able to use American dollars, and there is no need to change your money before departure.

Cape Eleuthera Villas, Yacht and Country Club

Cape Eleuthera
The Bahamas

Billed as a "three-million-dollar country club", Cape Eleuthera Villas is a very new, very modern, and very luxurious resort on Eleuthera, the prettiest of the Bahamian islands, and long a favorite watering hole of millionaires and celebrities. The reasons for Eleuthera's popularity are obvious. Beautiful uncrowded beaches, rocky cliffs, secret coves, coral reefs and undersea gardens all contribute to its popularity but the big drawing card has always been the deep-sea fishing. This area abounds in marlin, bonefish, amberjack, dolphin, snapper, and hundreds of other varieties of tropical fish. Fishermen come from all over North America for a chance to get at the big ones and docking facilities are excellent at the Cape Eleuthera Yacht Club.

The eighteen-hole golf course; fishing; scuba-diving; water skiing and sailing; all are well organized and close at hand, but for the tennis player, this is paradise.

There are six asphalt courts, a pro, and a pro-shop where equipment can be rented or bought. All the courts are lighted for night play. They have to be reserved a day ahead, but hotel guests do not have to pay for their use. Playing time depends on the demand, but getting enough time is usually not a problem. The most crowded months are from December to April. Cape Eleuthera Villas attracts mostly an over-forty clientele, interested in fishing and golf. However, a younger tennis crowd has recently made an appearance and this hotel might well become one of the most active tennnis spots in the Caribbean.

All accommodation is in villas, each with a bedroom, sitting room and a private verandah. Fresh fish, seafood and tropical fruit are the specialties here, as well as some extraordinary drinks which are concocted at the bar. This is a first-class hotel in the upper price bracket. For information on prices, write to the Reservations Manager.

The Montagu Beach Hotel
P.O. Box N 8308
Nassau, Bahamas

Often described as "somewhere between a European castle and an American hotel", the Montagu Beach has an old-world charm, which, combined with American efficiency makes it a wonderful spot for a holiday. The sprawling thirty-seven-acre complex once favored by royalty, visiting aristocracy, and the occasional movie star, has once again been restored to its original grandeur and is now considered the in place by many New Yorkers who can afford its stiff prices.

The Montagu has four Teniko-surface courts in first-class condition. The courts adjoin the hotel and are lighted for night play. The pro-shop sells a good range of tennis equipment and clothing. The tennis pro, Bradley Demeritte gives lessons and arranges round robins when there is a demand for them. Courts can be reserved one day in advance. There is a charge of $2.00 per hour per court. This is an active tennis spot with a good standard of tennis.

The hotel has a very pretty private beach. Boat rentals, water skiing, sailing, snorkeling and skin-diving equipment are all available on the hotel beach.

A large swimming pool is close to the tennis courts. The dining room is one of the most charming hotel dining rooms I have seen anywhere. Beautiful tropical foliage and candlelight complement the careful service and excellent food.

European-plan winter rates range from $26 to $38 double occupancy. This does not, of course, include meals. A modified American Plan (breakfast and dinner) is available on request.

A medium-size hotel of 176 rooms, The Montagu offers good value for money spent. For more information on rates write to the Manager.

Treasure Cay Beach Hotel
Abaco
The Bahamas

Treasure Cay is considered by many to be one of the most beautiful islands in the Bahamas. Known as "The Innocent Island", it has over three miles of broad, white beach facing a superbly clean multi-colored sea.

Fishing is the name of the game at Treasure Cay where the marina offers good anchorage and the sea is inhabited by some of the greatest fighting fish in the world.

A short walk from the hotel is the Treasure Cay Golf Course and Country Club. The golf course is rated as one of the three top courses in the Bahamas. It is a superb eighteen-hole Dick Wilson championship course with a new $500,000 clubhouse and restaurant.

Nestling in the quiet gardens of the Treasure Cay Beach Hotel is the Tennis Club; ten well kept courts (two clay, two asphalt, six acrylic finish), pro-shop and clubhouse. Tennis is a popular sport at Treasure Cay and this tennis club is by far the best organized in the Bahamas. Regular tournaments, clinics, private lessons and friendly round robins create an enthusiastic tennis atmosphere. Courts have to be reserved and playing time is limited to one hour. There is a charge of $1.00 per person per hour. Three of the courts are lighted for night play. A unique feature of the courts here is that you can choose to play either in the sunlight or in the shade provided by enormous pines which fringe the courts. After a few days of Bahamian sun, one

Donald Dell, the former U.S. Davis Cup Team Captain, playing with the Barbados champion during an exhibition match while Dell was on his honeymoon at the Barbados Hilton in the West Indies.

makes a run for the shady courts. All the courts are just off the beach and are constantly swept by air fresh from thousands of miles of open ocean. The pro here is Elbert Rolle, a well-known name in Bahamian tennis circles.

The pro-shop is completely equipped with the latest in tennis equipment and tennis fashions. Restringing is done on the premises. At Treasure Cay an informal and relaxed atmosphere prevails. Sports, not night life are the big attraction.

The Treasure Cay Beach Hotel and Villas is a very modern air-conditioned complex offering the very latest word in luxury living. Hotel rooms, beach villas and garden villas provide a choice of accommodations. The beach villas are the most luxurious and the most expensive. Overall rates range from $23 to $40 per person, Modified American Plan. Prices are slightly lower in the off season. For more information, write to their Florida office — Treasure Cay, 2801 Ponce de Leon Boulevard, Miami. The telephone number there is 444-8381-2.

The Barbados Hilton
Barbados
West Indies

The Barbados Hilton, a large well-run hotel in the Hilton tradition, is one of the few places in the Barbados where tennis is keen. It can get very hot here, even in January, and once hooked on leisurely island life, it is much easier to sit in the shade of a palm tree and sip a cool drink than to rush around a tennis court. However, at the Hilton, one will find people on the courts.

There are two grasstex courts, both lighted for night play. They are open from 8 a.m. to 10 p.m. every day. There is no charge to guests of the hotel during the daylight hours but there is a charge of $3.00 U.S. per hour after dark for use of the lights. The hotel has a full-time professional, Arthur Mapp, who charges $8.00 U.S. for an hour's lesson. Ball boys are available at $1.00 U.S. per hour and racquets can be rented from the pro-shop. The social hostess, Gercine Carter arranges games.

All the usual Caribbean sports and amusements are close at hand — fishing trips, snorkeling and skin diving expeditions, a golf course, beach, swimming pool, sightseeing tours and live evening entertainment. Calypso bands and singers are everywhere.

The outstanding culinary delights of Barbados are the mouth-watering tropical fruit and the fruit and rum punches. Night life is active on the island with many intimate Barbadian clubs well worth exploring.

The best time to come, and the most expensive, is from December to April. For information on rates, write to the Reservations Manager.

Coco Point Lodge
Barbuda
West Indies

The island of Barbuda, twenty-seven miles north of Antigua is a sportsman's paradise. The island itself abounds with birds, wild pigs and fallow deer, its waters with bonefish, tarpon and snook.

Barbuda is like no other island in the Caribbean. Coco Point Lodge is the only hotel on it. Barbuda's one town, Codrington, was originally a slave-breeding farm until the owner, Admiral Codrington, freed the slaves and gave them the town. Barbudians now eke a living from the lobster fishery and money from relatives living in New York and Toronto.

Seventy-three charted wrecks located among the reefs encircling the island provide a rich treasure trove for adventurers to explore. The Lodge is located on a 164-acre site with one and a half miles of fabulous white beach on the leeward side and a mile of waterfront on the windward side. To get to Coco Point Lodge you fly to Antigua and then by the hotel's private air service to a strip on the property. The flight from Antigua to Barbuda takes only ten minutes.

Activities at Coco Point Lodge are many and varied. Sailing (Sunfish), water skiing, scuba diving, snorkeling, reef fishing, horseback riding, hunting, deep-sea fishing, and yachting are all practically at your fingertips.

There is one all-weather tennis court with unlimited playing time. It is of course free. There is no pro or pro-shop, so bring your own equipment, and opponent, if you are an above-average player.

Coco Point Lodge operates on full American Plan. This includes not only all the food you can eat, but also all the wine and liquor you can drink. Lobster and other seafood delicacies enjoy their natural habitat in a netted Coco Point cove until they are ready to be eaten. Rumor has it that Princess Margaret honeymooned here.

Naturally, one has to pay to stay on this island paradise. Double accommodation, all meals and drinks included, ranges from $110 to $120 per day.

Delightfully unspoiled and surrounded by magnificent empty beaches, Barbuda and Coco Point Lodge are well worth a visit.

Auberge De La Vieille Tour

Gosier
Guadeloupe
French West Indies

To visit Guadeloupe is to step into a corner of provincial France which seems to be straight out of a Balzac novel. The climate, the vegetation, and the color of the skin may be different, but to drink *café au lait* in a courtyard overlooking a town square, takes you into another era and another way of life. When the sameness of Florida, the British Caribbean and Bermuda starts to pall, fly Air France to Guadeloupe. Here you will find the best food in the West Indies, a joie de vivre not usually associated with the Caribbean and an atmosphere of mystery; a feeling that there is a lot more going on than meets the eye.

The Auberge de la Vieille Tour is the most charming resort hotel on the island and it is only a twenty-minute drive from the airport in Pointe à Pitre. Built around an old sugar mill, it is now modernized and beautifully landscaped. Most rooms have terraces overlooking the sea and some of the sea views are magnificent. Many of the other guests are from France and are generally young and fun loving.

There is a small well-protected beach which is the center of activity during the day. Overlooking it is a small restaurant where one can linger over a leisurely lunch. The steak tartare and salad Nicoise are particularly good here.

The bar is located in the oldest part of the sugar mill and is a very lively and convivial spot. There is usually a small band for after-dinner dancing. An atmosphere of informality prevails and men do not have to wear jackets or ties. A knowledge of French is a real asset, both in the hotel and on the rest of the island.

Next to the swimming pool are three all-weather tennis courts. There is no pro or pro-shop and it is up to the tennis-playing guests to find each other. As the Auberge is a very friendly place, this is not difficult and many rousing games are the result. The caliber of tennis can, at best, be described only as average. Getting enough court time is never a problem.

Rent a car for a day and drive to the other end of the island to the historic capital of Guadeloupe, Basse Terre. Nearby is the Soufrière Volcano. It is interesting to note that while driving up the steep road which leads to the top of the volcano, the vegetation changes from tropical to a sort of scrub which is almost northern in appearance.

A double room, with breakfast and dinner costs approximately $60 for two. For the lover of French wines, this is the place to be — they are much cheaper here than in North America. One word of warning — it rains more in Guadeloupe than in most other Caribbean islands, but the rain generally doesn't last long, although completely overcast days are not unknown. For more information, write to the Manager.

Bay Roc

Montego Bay
Jamaica, W.I.

The Bay Roc is a large hotel facing the sea, located on the outskirts of Montego Bay, close to both the airport and to the town. Catering mostly to honeymooners and an over-thirty crowd, the Bay Roc is a busy informal place offering to its guests many activities and entertainments. There are both villa and hotel accommodations. The villas are located directly on

The Half Moon Hotel in Montego Bay, has seven laykold tennis courts, an eighteen-hole golf course, and one of Jamaica's most beautiful sandy beaches.

the beach and all hotel suites overlook the sea. The rooms are all air conditioned and have a private bath.

All water sports are available — water-skiing, scuba diving, snorkeling, glass-bottom boat rides and sailing. Prices for these activities vary, depending on the season. (Everything is much cheaper during the summer months.)

There is nightly entertainment in the form of dance bands, beach parties, floor shows, fashion shows, and of course, the ever-present calypso bands and singers.

There are two laykold tennis courts, unlit, which are free to hotel guests. A resident pro, Milton Russell, gives lessons and there are free weekly clinics. An expansion of the tennis facilities is planned. A small pro-shop completes the tennis picture. The best time to play is in the early morning or after four in the afternoon. As sudden showers are not uncommon in Jamaica, the laykold surface is ideal because it dries quickly.

Bay Roc is in the medium-price range. A double room, Modified American Plan costs from $48 to $68 per day. For more information concerning rates and package tours write to Jeanne Maitland, Reservations Manager.

Half Moon Hotel and Cottage Colony

Montego Bay
Jamaica, W.I.

The Half Moon is without a doubt one of the best places to stay when in Montego Bay. Nestled in a one-mile curve of white sandy beach are seventeen cottages, sixty-five rooms and suites, seven tennis courts and an eighteen-hole golf course. Each cottage has its own small swimming pool and there is another enormous free-form pool close to the tennis courts.

The golf course is a par 72, eighteen-hole course designed by Robert Trent Jones. It is a well manicured challenging course ranked among the best in the West Indies. Snorkeling and sailing are two other popular activities.

There are seven laykold tennis courts — unlit at the moment, but there are plans to install lights in at least four of them. Recently the hotel has obtained the services of the internationally known player Richard Russell as head professional, with Loxley Walters as assistant pro. Weekly hotel tournaments are a regular feature of the tennnis program, as are clinics. An extensive tennis program is being promoted here and the Half Moon will soon be an ideal tennis resort, as it is now an ideal golf resort. A new pro-shop (which does restringing), a gym and a bar are located next to the courts. A private half-hour lesson from Richard Russell costs $12.50; from Loxley Walters only $5.00. Guests do not pay for use of the courts but outsiders pay $2.00 per person per hour. The Half Moon hopes to stage celebrity and international tournaments in the near future. Ball boys are on hand to chase balls.

The dining room faces the sea and serves good American-type food. It features a quiet band for nightly dancing.

Be sure to visit Rose Hall which is very near to The Half Moon. This is an old restored plantation house with a gory past. Here you can have lunch in an English-style pub and wander around the house and garden.

The Half Moon is only a few minutes drive away from both the center of Montego Bay and the airport. From the tourist's viewpoint the town of Montego Bay is a conglomerate of hotels and duty-free shops. Beware of local native markets — you have to bargain to get good value. The Doctor's Cave Beach is the most active beach in Montego Bay. World famous for its natural beauty, it is well worth a visit.

The Half-Moon Hotel is in the luxury price range. Rates vary from $49 to $99 per day per double room, M.A.P. For further information concerning rates write to Mr. Peter Anthony Fraser, Resident Manager.

The Montego Bay Racquet Club

P.O. Box 245,
Montego Bay
Jamaica, W.I.

Set high on a hill overlooking Montego Bay, the Montego Bay Racquet Club provides an idyllic setting for the main preoccupation of its guests — playing tennis.

The Montego Bay Racquet Club in Jamaica offers a free tennis clinic to guests once a week.

The ten all-weather courts are all lighted for night play. A tennis professional, Bill Sturgess, or his assistant, Basil Thompson, are available for lessons all the year around. A half-hour lesson from Bill Sturgess costs $8.00. Games are arranged by the tennis hostess, Morna McLean, who also runs the pro-shop and sells very charming tennis dresses which she makes herself. Every Wednesday night at nine, a mixed-doubles round robin is staged which lasts far into the night. As partners are assigned by Bill Sturgess, the results are often hilarious. A rum punch freely distributed between rounds does not do much to improve one's game.

A free tennis clinic is given by Bill Sturgess once a week. Ball boys are automatically on hand at all times, and there is no charge either for them or for the use of the courts. Reservations cannot be made more than a day in advance. Doubles is the name of the game here. Singles are only tolerated early in the morning and late in the evening when court space is available.

Golfing, scuba diving, sailing, fishing, horseback riding and tours to all parts of the island can be arranged at the front desk. There is a shuttle service to and from the famous Doctor's Cave Beach, which is a two-minute drive away.

The Club, which has an excellent chef, offers an international cuisine with an exceptionally good buffet once a week which draws diners from all over Montego Bay. The climate is tropical, with the high season lasting from December through March.

Shopping forays into Montego Bay are popular between tennis games. Duty-free shops are everywhere, with bargains in cameras, perfumes, jewelry, English china, cashmeres and watches. Although the town and its attractions are but two minutes away, the ambiance of the Montego Bay Racquet Club is such that most guests seldom venture very far from either the tennis courts, the pool, the poolside bar or the pleasures of the table. As this is a very popular spot, reservations must be made well in advance and the same people come back year after year.

Guests are accommodated in fourteen cottages, nineteen rooms, and four luxury suites. Rates vary between $66 and $100 daily per double room, Modified American Plan. For more information write to the Reservations Manager.

Runaway Bay Hotel and Country Club

P.O. Box 58
Runaway Bay
Jamaica

The Runaway Bay Hotel and Country Club is particularly popular with the golfing crowd, as its two golf courses are renowned for their beauty and good design. It has two laykold tennis courts which are constantly in use and must be reserved ahead of time. There is no charge for use of the courts to hotel guests. The courts are lighted and ball boys are usually on duty.

A first-class hotel, catering to an over-thirty age group, Runaway Bay has one of the best chefs in Jamaica who is rightly famous for his sauces and meat dishes.

A beach, swimming pool, sailing, snorkeling, fishing and skin diving complete the sports picture. Snorkeling is extraordinarily good here; being slightly off the beaten track, the sea teems with every imaginable form of life. Deep-sea fishing is also better than average.

All rooms are large, air-conditioned and face the sea. For information on rates and special packages write to Mr. James N. Wright, Resident Manager.

Tower Isle Hotel

Ocho Rios
Jamaica

The Tower Isle Hotel is a first-rate resort hotel in Ocho Rios, a small town about a two-hour drive from the nearest airport in Montego Bay. Very popular with honeymooners, particularly from May to October, the Tower Isle has a very friendly and fun-loving group of people as its guests.

The beach at the Tower Isle is the best in the area. It is completely protected by a reef and has a little island facing it,

Although The Runaway Bay Hotel and Country Club is particularly noted for its golf courses, two lighted laykold tennis courts complete with ball boys are available for tennis enthusiasts.

which is great fun to explore and swim to. Sailing, snorkeling, water skiing and skin diving can all be arranged from the hotel beach. A large fresh-water filtered swimming pool is adjacent to the beach and lunches are served around it.

There is an eighteen-hole golf course at the Upton Country Club, five miles away from Tower Isle. There are two eighteen-hole championship golf courses at the Runaway Golf and Country Club, approximately twenty-five miles away from the hotel. These courses are open to guests of the Tower Isle.

Three laykold tennis courts are maintained by the hotel. Two of the courts are very new, and since their installation, tennis at the Tower Isle has become a much more popular and competitive sport than previously. There is no charge for use of the courts, but they do have to be reserved a day ahead of time. There is a tennis pro on the premises who gives both private lessons and tennis clinics. Racquets and balls can be obtained from the pro.

The hotel operates a very large resort shop which sells everything from free-port liquor to cameras. A beauty parlor, barber shop, post office and a boutique which sells children's and women's resort clothing complete the shopping facilities.

Ocho Rios is a small town of six thousand people with several interesting shopping areas. Good buys, besides the duty-free goods, are Jamaican-made dresses, bikinis, beads and straw products.

Outings to Dunn's Falls, rafting on the Rio Grande, and plantation tours although part of every tourist's routine in Ocho Rios, are nevertheless interesting and fun, especially on days when your sunburn will not let you lie on the beach.

Summer rates (from April 16 to December 15) Modified American Plan, start at $22.50 double, per person and go as high as $27.50. Winter rates range from $32.50 to $40.

The food is good hotel fare. Both the fresh fruit and fresh fish are outstanding. Also, the hotel goes out of its way to keep its guests entertained. Crab races, calypso singers, native floor shows, variety nights and dances are held constantly.

Jackets and ties must be worn for dinner, but otherwise an air of informality prevails. The Tower Isle has 141 double air-conditioned rooms with private balconies, and sixteen single rooms which are not air-conditioned and which are therefore much cheaper. For more information, write to the Reservations Manager.

Tryall Golf and Beach Club
Sandy Bay
Hanover, Jamaica

Located fourteen miles west of Montego Bay Airport, Tryall is a luxury development advertised as "Jamaica's finest resort". This claim is well founded. Visually it is certainly breathtaking. The hotel owns a total of three-thousand acres of waterfront and mountains. Members of the Tryall Golf and Beach Club have built approximately fifty two, three, and four-bedroom villas, most of which have their own pools, on a steep winding road going up the mountain. The architecture, the landscaping, and the views are all breathtaking. These villas are rented when their owners are not using them. Rentals can be arranged through the hotel; most villas are rented fully staffed.

At the bottom of the hill and on the other side of the road, are: the main house, (a beautifully restored 250-year-old plantation house), a large swimming pool with a bar, the tennis courts, the golf course, more cottages and the beach. The beach is the usual beautiful Caribbean beach, with good snorkeling areas nearby. The beach-side restaurant serves good light lunches. Their lobster salad is delicious.

There are four lighted laykold tennis courts, a professional, and a small pro-shop. More tennis courts and better tennis facilities are in the planning stages. Tennis is, of course, played all year around, but the winter is by far the best time to play, because of the extreme heat and humidity of the summer months.

The eighteen-hole golf course is a 6680-yard, par-71 championship course, reputed to be the best in the Caribbean.

Palm-lined trails which fringe the property are ideal for horseback riding. Sailing, sightseeing, and shopping in Montego Bay are other popular diversions.

The Tower Isle Hotel in Ocho Rios, Jamaica has three laykold tennis courts in a beautiful tropical setting.

There are fifty-two well-appointed guest rooms clustered around the main house. The main house contains some small shops, a bar, a lounge area and dining room. The dining room serves breakfast and dinner only. During the summer, dress is very informal, but in the winter a jacket and tie must be worn for dinner.

Tryall is not cheap. During the high season (December 16 to April 15) a double room, Modified American Plan starts at $83 a day and can go as high as $110, depending on its size and location. From April 16 to November 1, a double room can be had for only $42 to $55 per day. Tryall is truly a luxury resort in every sense of the word.

Aruba Caribbean Hotel—Casino

Aruba
Netherlands Antilles

At the Aruba Caribbean the accent is on efficiency and comfort. Everything that the Caribbean has to offer is practically within a stone's throw of the main lobby. The palm-fringed beach, the olympic-size swimming pool, air-conditioned bars and restaurants, rental fishing boats, the casino — are all within easy reach.

There are four all-weather tennis courts, a professional and a pro-shop which sells some equipment and tennis clothing, but does not really have a wide selection of either. The courts are lighted for night play, and although tennis is a popular sport, the two main preoccupations of the guests are the beach and the casino. Courts have to be reserved a day ahead.

The hotel offers a tennis program for groups, with very reasonable group rates. Reservations can be made through their New York office, Executive Houses Inc., 630 Fifth Avenue. (The telephone number is 212-265-7474.)

The food is good and the service is very friendly. Many interesting Dutch dishes are a welcome relief from the usual bland Caribbean fare. Rates, depending on the season, range from $18 to $30, Modified American Plan for a single room in the off season, to $35 to $53 for the same rooms in the high season (December 16 to April 29).

Aruba itself is a country of contrasts. The natives speak Dutch, English, Spanish and the musical Aruban language called Papiamento. There are many interesting villages, pirate coves, unusual trees, birds and flowers everywhere.

Little Bay Beach Hotel
St. Maarten
Netherlands Antilles

St. Maarten is a half-Dutch, half-French island not far from Puerto Rico or Antigua. Connections to St. Maarten can be made via KLM/ALM, Caribair, Air France, BWIA/LIAT and other major airlines, depending on the point of departure.

The island has an average temperature of eighty to eighty-five degrees F., but is cooled by constant trade winds. The vegetation is lush and tropical. It can and does rain at any time, but usually the clouds pass by quickly.

Over the years St. Maarten has been besieged not only by the French and Dutch, but also by the English and Spanish. Old forts give evidence of a long and interesting history. The quaint old-world buildings and tropical charm of the Dutch capital Phillipsburg, and the French capital Marigot, are interesting to explore after one tires of free-port shopping. Islanders in both areas generally speak some English and there are no regulations to hinder travel between the two sections.

The Little Bay Beach Hotel is a pleasant, smallish (120-room) modern resort. It is located directly on a lovely stretch of white sand and most of its rooms face the sea. The cuisine here is not as blandly international as in most Caribbean resorts, but offers some spicy West Indian and unusual Dutch delicacies.

Swimming either in the sea or in the fresh-water pool, sailing, skin diving, water skiing, and some of the world's finest sport fishing are all here.

A small casino, Casino Las Vegas, is on the premises and here you can gamble away your life savings at the roulette wheel, surrounded by every comfort and luxury.

Head tennis pro Nick Bollettieri coaching guest at the Cerromar Beach Hotel in Puerto Rico. Four full-time professionals offer daily lessons on Cerromar's six courts.

The hotel has three asphalt tennis courts built in 1973. All are lighted for night play. The tennis pro is Donald Cannegleter, a local talent, who has received professional training in the States. The tennis courts are free to guests, but at night there is a charge of $1.00 per hour for use of the lights. Tennis equipment is available for rental in the small pro-shop. Little Bay offers a tennis package from May 1 to December 20, which is excellent value and which includes a one-hour daily lesson from the pro.

Rates vary according to the season. In the high season (December 15 to May 1) the cost of a double room, Modified American Plan ranges from $65 to $74. There are suites for $79. Specify when making reservations whether you want a room facing the sea or the swimming pool. Beach-front rooms are of course more expensive. For more information write to Mr. Robert Dubourcq, Manager.

Cerromar Beach Hotel

P.O. Box 409
Dorado Beach
Puerto Rico 00646

The Cerromar Beach Hotel is an ocean-front resort, designed to take advantage of Puerto Rico's benevolent year-round climate. It is located a mile west of its companion resort, the Dorado Beach Hotel, and is situated on the 1700-acre Dorado resort and residential complex, twenty-two miles west of San Juan. The hotel has a total of 503 rooms designed in a double-Y configuration, so that guest rooms are along one side of the corridors only, thus providing each room with a view of the sea. All rooms are air conditioned and have private balconies. The six dining rooms are renowned throughout Puerto Rico for the excellence of their food; their chefs have won many international prizes.

Recreational facilities include two eighteen-hole championship golf courses, thirteen all-weather laykold tennis courts, a 1600-foot beach, an olympic-size swimming pool, a children's playground, a casino, men's and women's health clubs and saunas, a night-club and all the water sports. The hotel is open all the year around, with off-season rates effective from April 1 to December 20.

Nick Bollettieri is the head pro of the Tennis Club. There are two assistant pros, Orlando Cruz and Jim Nerren. Private lessons vary in price between $15 and $25 per hour. A complete pro-shop with restringing facilities is on the premises. The courts do not have lights and they must be reserved one day ahead. Guest court fees are $1.50 per day from October 20 to May 1 and $1 from May 1 to October 20. Clinics and friendly tournaments are regular features.

Rates are Modified American Plan. A double room in the winter season costs from $90 to $100. The same room in the summer costs only $55 to $60. There are many special golf, tennis and honeymoon packages. The Cerromar is an excellent place for children as they are kept busy and amused in a free children's day camp. For more information write to the Reservations Manager.

Dorado Beach Hotel
Dorado Beach
Puerto Rico

The Dorado Beach Hotel is twenty miles west of San Juan and three miles from the town of Dorado. It has a total of three-hundred rooms in separate beach houses and cabanas. These are ranged along two crescent beaches on either side of a central building containing lounge areas, dining rooms and terraces, function rooms, casino, and shops. *Fielding's Guide to the Caribbean*, 1971 edition, states that the Dorado has the best food in the Caribbean. Their executive chef, Alfred Fahndrich is considered the best chef in Puerto Rico.

Nestled within its fifteen-hundred acres are two eighteen-hole Robert Trent Jones designed golf courses, seven laykold tennis courts, tropical forests and citrus groves, two miles of ocean frontage, and excellent beaches. Activities here include swimming in the sea or in salt-water pools, snorkeling, water skiing, sailing, golf, tennis, fishing, and bicycling. Carriage rides, beach

Chris Evert playing at the Cerromar Beach Hotel in Puerto Rico, which provides guests with six all-weather tennis courts, two eighteen-hole championship golf courses, a 1600-foot beach and an olympic-size swimming pool

parties, dinner dances, air tours to nearby Caribbean islands, and sightseeing and shopping in historic San Juan are also popular.

There are seven all-weather tennis courts here. Nick Bollettieri is the head tennis pro both at the Dorado and its sister hotel, the Cerromar. He and his assistant pro, Gewan Maharaj, give lessons, arrange games and stage guest tournaments. A one-hour private lesson costs $25. Court fees for guests of Dorado Beach are $2 per person per hour. There is a well equipped pro-shop with restringing facilities and racquet rentals. The Dorado is the home of the Dorado Beach and Tennis Club, a private club with many of its members permanent residents of San Juan. Consequently, getting enough court time can be a problem.

The Dorado Beach Hotel is operated on the Modified American Plan. Substantially reduced rates are in effect from April 1 to December 20 of each year. There are many special packages which are very good value. For more information write to Mr. Gene Tinker, Reservations Manager.

Hotel Racquet Club

Isla Verde
San Juan
Puerto Rico

The Hotel Racquet Club, located in the center of the San Juan tourist area, is a 250-room, off-the-beach hotel with excellent tennis facilities. There are eight cork-turf championship courts, four of which are equipped with lights for night play. Guests of the hotel may use the courts free of charge, but the courts have to be reserved a day ahead. There is a charge of $5 per hour per court for night play. The tennis pro is Yvan Martinez, who gives lessons at the rate of $12 per half hour. A complete pro-shop (with restringing facilities) and a clubhouse are part of the tennis complex. Tennis is the main activity at the Racquet Club and the caliber of play is high.

There is a racquet-shaped swimming pool next to the courts where one can cool off after a fast set. The beach is only a few minutes' walk away, and several golf courses are in the area. The hotel offers nightly entertainment, dancing, and an international cuisine. Old San Juan with its lovely old-world architecture, its many small shops and its restaurants is nearby and is well worth exploring. European Plan rates vary according to season and type of accommodation, starting at $23 for a double room in the off season (summer) and going up to $35 in the winter season. For more information write to Ms. Marsha Tursi, Manager.

Palmas Del Mar

Puerto Rico

The Sea Pines Company, developer of Sea Pines Plantation in Hilton Head, South Carolina, has just built a resort complex on the southeastern coast of Puerto Rico, comprising several villages clustered among coves and beaches overlooking the Caribbean, approximately one hour's drive from San Juan. A harbor complex has been designed along the lines of a Mediterranean village and this is the major center of activity at Palmas.

The tennis village is nestled in a hillside overlooking both the Caribbean and the mountains. Here there will eventually be approximately forty tennis courts and an amphitheatre accommodating 2,500 spectators. The NBC Family Circle Cup Tournament is scheduled here for 1974. The tennis facilities at Palmas will probably be the most complete and most modern in the world. A variety of court surfaces have been built to suit every taste. Charles Pasarell is the Tennis Director. He will be making frequent visits to Palmas for clinics, exhibition matches and tournaments. Jim Osborne, a former member of the U.S. Davis Cup Squad, has been appointed resident professional.

A beach village, combined with fairways and greens of the first of three eighteen-hole golf courses, is in the middle of a hundred-and-fifty-acre grove of fifty-foot coconut palms and is surrounded by several miles of crescent beaches.

At Palmas there is also an equestrian center, a tropical conservatory with a thousand-foot broadwalk wandering through a jungle of orchids. There are bicycle, riding, and hiking trails

Tom Hauser, the resident tennis professional, giving lessons at the Pineapple Beach Resort on the island of St. Thomas in the Virgin Islands.

along the coastline and coves and beaches for snorkeling and swimming. Accommodations are in The Palmas Inn, town houses around the tennis village or in condominiums throughout the property. Lots are still available for sale around the tennis, beach and harbor villages.

For more information, write to Barbara Kappler, Manager, Palmas del Mar, Sales and Information Center, 207 Harbor House, Hilton Head, S.C. 29228.

Pineapple Beach Resort

P.O. Box 2516
St. Thomas
U.S. Virgin Islands

Located four miles northeast of Charlotte Amalie, the capital of U.S. Virgin Islands, and the only town on St. Thomas, Pineapple Beach Resort offers the following facilities, services and accommodations: a one-thousand-foot private, white-sand beach, 185 air-conditioned rooms, two large fresh-water swimming pools, a beach and pool bar, tropical buffets and barbecues, nightly dancing and entertainment, all water-sports including sailing and snorkeling instruction on the beach, charter arrangements for cruises, and fishing aboard the yacht *Pineapple* and free-port gift shops.

The weather in St. Thomas is tropical, ranging from seventy-five to ninety degrees F. in the winter and eighty to ninety-five degrees F. in the summer.

There are three cork-turf courts here, two of which are lighted for night play. Thomas F. Hauser is the professional and is available for instruction six days a week from 9 a.m. to 7 p.m. A ball-boy machine is available for rental. There is no charge for use of the courts for hotel guests, but visitors have to pay a small fee. The light fee is $4.00 per hour. A complete pro-shop with changing and showering facilities is situated next to the courts. Courts must be reserved and playing time is limited to one hour. Local residents also play here, which means that the caliber of tennnis is high, but getting enough court time can be a problem.

The price of accommodation varies with type of room and season. From May 1 to December 21, double rooms, Modified American Plan cost from $54 to $62. The same rooms from December 22 to May 1 cost from $68 to $78. Two bedroom beach houses and one and two bedroom suites are also available. For more information write to Ms. Maria Hauser, Reservations Manager.

CHAPTER 4
ENGLAND

The compelling variety of exciting sights in London — museums, restaurants, theaters, markets, shops — makes it difficult to move on to the sporting aspects of one's holiday. If money is no object, stay at Claridge's or the Connaught and savor to the full the elegance and ease of London at its best. Once you are able to extricate yourself from this city, the countryside offers beautiful scenery which is full of contrasts and historic places.

The weather in Britain is never reliable, but June is a fairly good bet. Wimbledon is on for the tennis afficionado and it is also the month for Ascot and the Antique Dealer's Fair.

It is a myth that the food is bad in England. Not only are there a multitude of excellent French and Italian restaurants in London, but generally, the quality of English cuisine is high. The food is straightforward and carefully prepared. It is not the most imaginative cuisine, but the very fresh vegetables and dairy products and the well-hung meat more than compensate. Fish and lamb are abundant and very good. Afternoon tea is a lovely treat everywhere and the time should be taken to enjoy it.

For variety of shopping, England is the best in Europe — both haute couture as well as inexpensive men's, women's and children's clothing; leather goods from wallets to suitcases; woolens and linens; fabrics; home furnishings; antiques, and china. Remember to take advantage of the Personal Export Scheme to avoid purchase tax if you are doing a lot of serious shopping.

The pound is worth approximately $2.40 and there are 42 p. to the dollar. To get into England you must have a passport, but you do not need a vaccination certificate if coming from North America.

Forest Park Hotel

Brockenhurst
Hampshire SO472G
England

One of the few areas of still unspoilt land left in England is found in the south. This is the 100,000 acres known as the New Forest. Situated in one corner of the Forest is the Forest Park Hotel. A visiting journalist describes his impressions of the hotel: "It has an atmosphere you could carve off in slices and take away with you. The highly polished mahogany, the deep reds, the plush leather, the wrought iron and copper, the intimacy of the cocktail bar and restaurant, combine to produce the kind of feeling you get from drinking a good brandy — it begins inside."

The thirty-three rooms are heated and most rooms have their own baths. There is a dinner dance every Saturday night, but the general trend is to let the guests relax and not to organize them in any way. The dining room overlooks the grounds and swimming pool. The food here is typically country-English. Attractions include riding stables and ideal riding conditions in the nearby Forest, and the New Forest golf courses. A new eighteen-hole course has been built at the New Forest Golf Club in Lyndhurst, only a few miles away. This is a very friendly club and welcomes visitors. A similar type of club is Bramshaw, where the eighteen-hole golf course is again set in the New Forest. The natural hazards here are ponies, cattle and deer. They have the right of way.

There is one hard tennis court on the hotel property. The hotel can, if required, produce a tennis professional for lessons. There is no charge for use of the court and playing time is unlimited. A sauna after a fast set is a good way to relax.

The New Forest has some of the most famous salmon and trout streams in England. Amid the quiet serenity of the Forest many pleasant afternoons can be whiled away in search of a good trout for the next day's breakfast. The sea is not far away and outings to the beaches of Bournemouth are arranged by the hotel.

Beaulieu, one of England's most popular stately homes, the Compton Acres Gardens and the Isle of Wight are interesting places to visit. Of course the New Forest itself is endlessly fascinating with its natural beauty and wildlife.

A double room with bath, and all meals included, costs approximately $25 a day. For more information write to Mr. D. E. Lancombe, Manager.

Gabriel Court Hotel

Stoke Gabriel, near Totnes
South Devon
England

Stoke Gabriel, with its ancient fishing rights, is a quaint and picturesque village, three miles from the railway station at Paignton. An old manor house which until recently has been in the possession of one family since 1485, the Gabriel Court Hotel is situated in the peaceful village of Stoke Gabriel on the banks of the Dart River. It stands in a terraced Elizabethan garden of archways, magnolia trees, and a high surrounding wall and occupies approximately three acres.

All rooms are heated and most of them face south. Ten of the twenty-six rooms have private bathrooms. The hotel welcomes children; cots, high chairs, separate meal-times and baby sitters are readily available. Gabriel Court has a reputation for good English cooking, which is well deserved. Fruit and vegetables (in season) are from their own vegetable garden, salmon and sea trout are freshly caught in the Dart, and poultry comes from neighboring farms. There is a very pleasant bar and the wine cellar stocks moderately priced but carefully chosen wines. The beer is, of course, far superior to American beer.

The Churston eighteen-hole golf course and riding stables are only two miles away. A children's attraction is the Paignton Zoo. Fishing and river trips on the Dart are popular excursions. There are also many safe beaches and quiet coves nearby.

The hotel has one excellent grass tennis court, which is available to hotel guests free of charge. It is playable from April until late September. Tennis enjoys great popularity in England

and many rousing games are played here. If more competition is desired, the hotel will introduce its guests to the local tennis club.

A reasonably priced hotel, with a quiet country atmosphere, the Gabriel Court Hotel is far away from the usual tourist haunts. For more information write to Mr. O. M. Beacom, Manager.

Great Fosters
Egham, Surrey
England

Once a hunting lodge in the Royal Forest of Windsor owned by Elizabeth I, Great Fosters is now a four-star luxury hotel only nineteen miles from London. The hotel is forty-years old and boasts a clientele of princes, socialites, and movie stars. Its decor consists of period furniture, ornate plaster ceilings, oak paneling and unusual wood carving. The banqueting room is a fifteenth-century Tithe Barn where a dinner dance is held every Saturday. Accommodation is in suites and bedrooms furnished in styles contemporary with the house. All rooms have central heating and many have private bathrooms. A swimming pool is on the premises.

Great Fosters is surrounded by historical sites — Runnymede, Windsor Castle, Eton, Hampton Court Palace, Oxford and Stoke Poges, to mention just a few. Also, it is near to Ascot and Epsom, to the Wentworth and Sunningdale golf courses, and Wimbledon.

The hotel itself has only one hard tennis court, but there is no charge for its use and no limit on playing time. Plans are afoot to build more courts, as the demand for tennis facilities is constantly increasing.

A recent guest describes his arrival at Great Fosters: "I arrived at 1:30 a.m. and asked for a ham sandwich and a bottle of Bass. They were carefully produced, freshly made and freshly poured respectively and set out in front of a still cheerful log fire in the lounge." This comment describes the quality of service at Great Fosters, where the rates, taking in consideration value for money, are still quite reasonable. For more information write to The Manager.

The Lygon Arms

Broadway
Worcestershire, England

Broadway is probably the most famous village in England. It has lovely stone houses, mellow, unspoilt and dating back centuries. The Lygon Arms is no exception. It has provided shelter to travelers for more than four-hundred years, and is an example of an English country inn at its best. The first official mention of the Inn is in the Broadway Parish Records of 1532. Tradition has it that Oliver Cromwell slept in a first-floor room before the Battle of Worcester in 1651. This Cromwell room is today much as it was then, with a carved Elizabethan fireplace, an early seventeenth-century plaster-enriched ceiling and frieze, and genuine period furniture.

Charles I also stayed here on one of his many visits to Broadway and the room named after him still has the original seventeenth-century paneling. The room itself is approached by a spiral oak staircase. Of course, over the years there has been modernization but the new has been very cleverly melded with the old.

The surrounding Cotswold hills are ideal walking country and here one can walk for miles without tiring of the sights, sounds and smells of the English countryside at its best.

The less energetic will find Lygon Arms a convenient base for forays into historic England. There are many stately homes in the area open to visitors — Sulgrave Manor, the sixteenth-century ancestral home of George Washington's family whose crest, which is contained in a stained-glass window there, became the basis of the Stars and Stripes. On the way, stop at Banbury for its Cross and Cakes. Visit Oxford, and stop at Blenheim, home of the late Sir Winston Churchill. Warwick Castle, Coventry Cathedral and the cathedrals of Worcester are well worth seeing. When you have had your fill of history, come back to hearty English cooking and rich dark ale in the Tudor dining room of the Lygon Arms.

Sports activities such as golf, swimming, and horseback riding are easily arranged and are close at hand. The hotel has one hard tennis court, available to guests free of charge. Playing time is unlimited, and the season, depending always on the uncertain weather, lasts from April to October.

A double room with bath costs approximately $30 a night, without meals. Broadway is ninety miles from London and is easily accessible by rail.

Selsdon Park Hotel

Selsdon Park
Sanderstead
South Croydon
Surrey 2 8YA
England

The earliest record of what is now the Selsdon Park Hotel has been traced back to 861 A.D. when the Saxon, Duke Aelfrid bequeathed the "mansion on a hill" to his wife. Centuries later, the Templars held Selsdon for their overlord, the Archbishop of Canterbury and collected tithes in his name. Towards the end of the last century the old walls were encased in red brick and many additions were made before its conversion to a hotel in 1925.

The surrounding two-hundred acres of parkland boast many magnificent trees, and even though nobody has claimed that Queen Elizabeth I slept here, there is a majestic Lebanon cedar which, legend has it, was planted by Elizabeth on one of her visits to Selsdon.

Only ten miles from Wimbledon, the hundred-and-eighty-bedroom hotel has two all-weather and two grass courts. Derek B. Nicholls, resident professional, is also the principal director of England's largest nationally operated tennis school, the Lawn Tennis School, and together with his team of professionals, offers a wealth of expertise to the beginner and experienced player alike.

This hotel is one of the few large privately owned hotels left in the British Isles and it has been in the same family since its conversion. In addition to very good standards of accommodation, cuisine and service, the hotel has a wide range of other sporting amenities besides tennis. For golfers, there is an eighteen-hole golf course with resident professional Bill Mitchell. An outdoor heated swimming pool is open throughout the spring and summer months. For the riding enthusiast, there are a number of excellent trails over the estate.

Rates are dependent on length of stay, but start at $12 a day, including breakfast. A weekend at Selsdon is a very pleasant way to spend a quiet but sporty few days away from the London crowds.

Manolo Orantes and Ramon Munoz playing in an exhibition match at Lew Hoad's Campo de Tenis in Spain.

CHAPTER 5
EUROPE

AUSTRIA

Austria is scenically one of Europe's most beautiful countries and one of the least expensive for visitors. The Tyrol is ethnically the most interesting part of the country and boasts a marvellously healthy climate. At Innsbruck, the capital of the Tyrol, Maria Theresia Street with its arch of triumph, the Golden Roof in the middle of the old town, the Imperial Palace, the Imperial Church, and the Silver Chapel are worth seeing.

Of interest to shoppers are the typically Tyrolean articles; hats, loden cloth, handwoven materials, dirndls, lederhosen, leather clothing and wood carvings are all fairly reasonable in price.

Igls is a thousand feet above Innsbruck and in addition to playing tennis, one can swim in the Lanser See, about a mile away and hike in the Alps. The view from the top of Patscherkofel Mountain (get there by cable car) should not be missed.

There are seventeen to eighteen Austrian schillings to the dollar. It is customary to tip in Austria, although service is already added to the bill.

Club Igls

Igls
Tyrol
Austria

Located four miles from Innsbruck in the heart of the Austrian Alps, Club Igls is a tennis lover's paradise. Nine clay courts are available for the Club Igls program, which includes unlimited tennis, daily group instruction, and free use of tennis machines. One court is reserved for every six people. Private lessons are available at extra cost. Names on the teachers' rostrum include Fred Kovaleski, Valerie Zeigenfus, Chuck McKinley, and Tommy Burke. The program has been planned by

Bill Talbert. There is a social host and hostess on hand at all times. They arrange games and dispense hospitality.

Other sports available in the area are: recreational summer skiing with instruction at enormous discounts from top Austrian ski instructors, horseback riding, golf, swimming and indoor ice skating. Health-spa facilities are on the premises of the Sport Hotel. There is lots of night life in Innsbruck.

Accommodations are at the Sport Hotel in Igls, a very pleasant, smallish, typically Tyrolean hotel with a hearty Austrian cuisine and a friendly atmosphere.

The cost of this tennis package is $300 per week — six nights and seven days. The price includes all tennis instruction, court fees, and rooms with breakfast and dinner or lunch. The plan operates from June 1 to September 30.

For more information write to Mr. Andrew J. Stern, 357 East 57 Street, New York, N.Y. 10022, or telephone (212) 355-1385.

FRANCE

The Cote d'Azur, from Marseilles to Menton, lives up to its romantic name; hot Mediterranean sun, cloudless days that know no rain cooled by the mysterious mistral. It is a very busy coast, best avoided in August when the French all take their holidays and descend *en masse*, but one can go there comfortably anytime after Easter.

Most of the coastline is at the foothills of the Maures and Esterel mountain masses, and there are many spectacular drives along the steep cliffs that plunge into the sea. The countryside behind Cannes and Nice is one of rolling hills with deep canyons. The most famous is the Gorge de Verdon, which is one of the world's natural wonders. The town of Moustiers is nearby where the pottery of the same name with its exquisite handpainted designs, is still manufactured. It is also possible to find Moustiers pottery in souvenir shops along the coast.

Other excursions from Cannes, should include Vence, a delightful old market town, and St. Paul where the Maeght Museum contains some of the best works of Calder, Kandinsky, Giacommetti, Matisse and Chagall.

From Bandol at the western end of the Cote d'Azur one should visit the fortified medieval village of Le Castellet about twelve kilometers inland, where there are many antique and craft shops, good restaurants and concerts during the summer months.

Aix-en-Provence, the capital of Provence, is a beautiful city with its wide avenues, seventeenth and eighteenth century houses and squares still intact. There are excellent restaurants in Aix and very good shopping in a multitude of high-quality boutiques. From Bandol there are also boat excursions to the Calanques of Cassis.

Provencal cooking is sublime; the ratatouille, bouillabaisse and aioli, are a constant delight.

There are approximately four French francs to the dollar. A passport is usually required to change traveler's checks, often a time-consuming process, which can be simplified by buying one's traveler's checks in francs before departure. Everything in France, with the exception of wine and cheese, is expensive.

Club Montfleury

Parc François André
Avenue Beauséjour
06400 — Cannes
France

The Club Montfleury is the center of tennis activity in the Cannes area. It is a private club, but guests of the Mont Fleury Hotel and the Majestic can become temporary members for a fee of six francs (approximately $1.50) which entitles them to the use of the courts and the swimming pool at lower prices.

There are nine clay and one hard court. During the high season (spring and summer) they have to be reserved a day in advance and playing time is limited to forty-five minutes. In the fall and winter months courts can be reserved for the same day. Also, in the off season the charge is only twenty francs for forty-five minutes, compared to forty francs for the same time in the high season. There is a full complement of professionals, but be sure to ask for one who speaks English. A popular tournament for amateurs is held in June. Other tournaments are scattered throughout the year. A well-stocked pro-shop, shower and changing rooms are all on the premises.

The Club also runs an excellent restaurant where it is very easy to linger over two-hour lunches which often have the effect of inhibiting one's desire to play tennis in the afternoon.

The Hotel Mont Fleury is a very pleasant hotel with magnificent views of the sea and a very pretty garden. There are 130 rooms, most with their own bathroom. The Cannes Municipal Casino is nearby.

The Hotel Majestic is larger, with three-hundred rooms. It is situated on the *croisette*, and, as the beach has recently been thoroughly cleaned and reorganized, this is a distinct advantage during the swimming season. However, the Mont Fleury does have a swimming pool.

The attractions of the Riviera are too well known for us to delve into them here. Let us just say that for North Americans, the fabulous *quality* of the articles for sale, whether clothes, silver, jewelry, or objets d'art is a constant surprise. Nothing is cheap in France, but the quality of the workmanship and of the raw materials are without peer.

Eating is a favorite occupation of visitors and many delightful excursions combining sightseeing, visits to art galleries and shopping can be planned around a super meal at one of the many restaurants and country inns in the area.

For more information write to the Manager, Club Montfleury.

Hotel Royal

74502 *Evian*
France

Only forty-five kilometers from Geneva Airport, the Hotel Royal is well known as a water spa. Many claims for the health-giving properties of its waters have been made. The Thermal Establishment is part of the hotel and it also has facilities for medical and dietetic treatments.

The Hotel Royal is definitely a deluxe hotel. Located in the center of its own large park and surrounded by flowering terraces, it overlooks the Lake of Geneva and provides its guests with every comfort and luxury. A large, white, many-balconied building of roughly 1930s vintage, it has outstandingly beautiful public rooms. The main dining room and lobby have intricately painted and domed ceilings which accent the elegance of the hotel.

It is open from May to September, and besides health seekers, sport-minded people come here for the sailing, tennis, golf and horseback riding. A heated swimming pool is directly accessible from all the rooms, so that guests do not have to wander through the dignified lobby wearing their bathing suits. In typically civilized European fashion, there is also a casino and a night club on the premises.

Six clay tennis courts are situated on the hotel grounds. Three more are nearby at the golf course. A professional staff gives lessons, conducts clinics and arranges games. Most of the teaching staff speak some English, but any attempt at French is greatly appreciated. There is a small charge for use of the courts, which have to be reserved at least a day ahead. A well stocked pro-shop with restringing facilities is available to guests. For more information write to the Manager.

Sheraton Du Cap Hotel

20-*Ajaccio*
Porticcio
Corsica, France

Corsica, one of the largest islands in the Mediterranean, is a province of France. Just eight miles from Sardinia, it is 114 miles long and forty-two miles wide. Its population is 280,000. Almost a thousand miles of sandy beaches; bays and tiny hidden coves; Mediterranean towns and white secret villages perched on mountain tops — this is Corsica. Fir, beech and chestnut trees mingle with caneapples and myrtles. A mountainous country, one can ski in the mountains at Col de Vergio one day and come down to sea level and play tennis on the next.

Ajaccio is the capital town. With a resident population of fifty thousand, it is now primarily a resort town. Napoleon's birthplace, the Old Port, the old town, and the Corsican Ethnological

Museum are well worth seeing. Ajaccio is full of small restaurants, bars and cabarets. There is also an active tennis club here, to which the Sheraton du Cap will gladly arrange introductions for its guests.

The Sheraton du Cap Hotel is perched spectacularly on a rock on the south side of the Bay of Ajaccio offering magnificent views in all directions. It is only a ten-minute drive from the center of town. There are one-hundred rooms on two floors, each room with its own bathroom and terrace. Considered by many to be the best hotel in Corsica, it has its own heated pool, private beaches and tennis courts. Although not primarily a tennis resort, a decent game can always be rounded up. For more competitive tennis, one goes into town.

Fishing, sunbathing, eating, and taking the cure at the hotel health spa are favorite occupations. Prices for Modified American Plan (room, breakfast, dinner) range from 105 to 130 francs per person per day in the off season (April 15 to May 31, September 15 to October 31), to 135 and 170 francs in the high season (June 1 to September 14). One franc is worth approximately 25 cents.

Corsica has only recently become a tourist mecca; hence Corsicans are still friendly, interested and anxious to please. Plan to see it before their hospitality wears thin. Air France flies to Corsica from points in France, as well as from London.

Tennis-Hotel Buding

83 — Bandol
France

At the Tennis-Hotel Buding, there are more tennis courts, more tennis players, and more enthusiasm for the game than practically anywhere else. Certainly there is no larger or more complete complex in Europe.

Owned, staffed, and run by three Budings — Lothar, Edda, and Ilse, all internationally known tennis players, this is a resort with the facilities of both tennis camp and resort hotel. There are thirty fast-surface (hard) courts, four of which are lit for night play. As there is only accommodation for one-hundred people, getting enough court time is not a problem.

The Budings pride themselves on running a tight ship and just about everyone leaves the establishment with aching muscles, but with an improved tennis game. All the latest teaching aids are used — ball machines, video replays, warm-up exercises and clinics for all ages and levels of ability. There is stiff competition among the players. Tennis is taken very seriously and non-playing guests are rare.

A swimming pool, bar, boutique and a very good restaurant are the other amenities here.

There is a variety of accommodation, ranging from a room without bath for 55 francs ($16.50) a day with breakfast, to apartments sleeping five people for 140 francs ($42.00) a day. There are also special packages and children's rates, prices depending on the season and length of stay.

The Hotel Buding, besides offering an exceptional tennis program, is beautifully situated on the Bay of Bandol overlooking the Côte d'Azur. It is set in a grove of pine trees, which provide some shade from the heat of the Mediterranean summer sun.

A knowledge of French or German is a definite asset, but there are enough pros who speak English to get by with just English. The majority of guests are German and French.

This part of France is full of unbelievably good restaurants, luxury shops, Roman ruins and walled towns waiting to be explored. One word of advice — make your reservations well in advance. The popularity of both tennis and the Tennis-Hotel Buding is growing every year.

For more information, write to Mr. Lothar Buding, Manager.

Monte Carlo Country Club

Monte Carlo
Principality of Monaco

To play tennis at the Monte Carlo Country Club is to play under ideal conditions almost the whole year around. Not only the weather, but facilities and other players generate a very

The Monte Carlo Country Club, in the Principality of Monaco, has twenty tennis courts, two squash courts, a swimming pool and a clubhouse in an idyllic setting overlooking the Mediterranean.

keen tennis atmosphere. The sun shines more than three-hundred days a year, and while here, it is difficult to get upset about one's faulty serve, inconsistent backhand or non-existent overhead smash. Tennis can be enjoyed because even the casual visitor soon succumbs to the many charms of Monaco, and particularly to those of the Monte Carlo Country Club.

There are twenty tennis courts, two squash courts, a swimming pool and a clubhouse equipped with showers, pro-shop, and a very fine restaurant which faces the sea. The courts have a variety of surfaces. They are clay, grass, and hard, but all are kept in top-notch condition. Many tournaments are staged here and there is a large grandstand overlooking two of the clay courts for this purpose. There are three resident professionals who give individual instruction only. The Club also has all the most modern game improvement equipment.

The courts are open to visitors for $5 an hour. Guests of either the Hotel de Paris or L'Hermitage pay only $3 an hour. Courts have to be booked ahead, but playing time is practically unlimited, particularly from October to June.

The Club offers a tennis package of seven nights, seven days which includes all the tennis you can play, two private half-hour lessons, free entry to the Monte Carlo Casino and other lesser privileges. The price of this package varies from $177 at L'Hermitage in the off season (October to June) to $294 at the Hotel de Paris in the high season. All accommodations are Modified American Plan.

These two hotels are affiliated with the Tennis Club. Both offer excellent accommodation, with the Hotel de Paris being the more de luxe of the two. The Hotel de Paris is *the* established hotel of the area, and as is usual with European hotels of this quality, offers only the best in rooms, service and food. The Bar is a famous meeting place for all the in-people in Monaco.

L'Hermitage, the other hotel, is smaller, quieter and not as opulent. Prices are lower, although it is still a first-class hotel.

The Casino, the Opera, the Black Jack Club, the beach, and golf at the Monte Carlo Golf Club are all popular diversions.

For more information write to Mr. Roland Bourge at the Monte Carlo Country Club.

ITALY

The important fact to grasp about Italy is that the north is almost a different country from the south. Rome is the dividing point. In broad terms, it may be said that the north is more aristocratic, European, cosmopolitan, industrialized and wealthier, but that the essence of the Italian spirit is really in the south.

From Palladio's Roman revival Villa Rotunda in Vicenza, to the classic Greek temples at Paestum, Italy is dotted with innumerable monuments of all the great ages of architecture.

In the north, the lake district (Lakes Como, Garda and Maggiore) with its towns and beautiful Renaissance buildings, offers some of the most spectacular scenery in Europe. Or one can spend time in the ancient, exotic cities of Venice and Florence absorbing centuries of painting and sculpture in their museums. In the south, the most outstanding natural scenery is the Amalfi Drive, but that coast is terribly crowded in the summer. However, Corsica and Ischia are havens from the madding crowd.

Italian food is a delight and is quite different from the North American version that we are subjected to on this continent. In the north try *involtini* and *saltimbocca*. Southern cuisine is characterized by plentiful use of olive oil, garlic, and tomatoes. The pasta is always fresh and totally different from North American packaged varieties. Often it is best *al beurro*, although the sauces are tempting. Italians do not make a variety of sweets, but the *gelati* are excellent and all one needs after a full dinner. The best wines are found in the north near the French border, but anywhere in the country the wine is eminently potable.

The shopping in Italy is wonderful. Every decent-sized town has a market; the one in Florence is especially good. Some of the better buys are silks, shoes, handbags, and gold jewelry. Italian fashions are very stylish and the quality of workmanship is excellent. Milan is the center of modern-design furniture and accessories.

The weather is predictably fine, although it can be very hot

The Regina Isabella Hotel, on the island of Ischia, off Italy, offers two well-maintained clay courts and regularly organized tournaments for hotel guests.

in mid-summer. It is important to check on pollution before venturing in swimming near the big northern centers. There are approximately 595 lira to the dollar.

Cristallo Palace
42 *Via Menardi*
Cortina d'Ampezzo
Italy

Scene of the jet set's revels in the winter, the Cristallo Palace is an oasis of peace and quiet in the summer months. Overlooking the Cortina valley with a spectacular view of the Dolomites, the Cristallo is a beautiful, old fashioned hotel of one-hundred rooms. However, it does have all the latest modern conveniences. Every room is individually furnished with antiques and oriental rugs. Freshly cut flowers are everywhere.

There are two clay courts at the Cristallo. The courts are not lighted. They are open from 8 a.m. to 8 p.m. from May to the end of September. A fee of $1.75 per person per hour is charged for use of the courts. The professional is Milan Mathous who charges $4 per half-hour lesson. Although there is no clubhouse, the swimming pool area is immediately adjacent to the courts. It has a bar and restaurant.

Two big tournaments are held here every year — a veteran's tournament during the first two weeks in July and the Senior Tournament during the latter part of August. These are very popular and draw a large number of entries and many spectators. Tennis at the Cristallo, despite the fact that there are only two courts, is very keen. Reservations for courts must be made a day in advance.

The Monkey Night Club featuring a discothèque and grill is the most popular and most crowded night club in Cortina. Golf, horseback riding, mountain climbing, hiking or exploring ruined castles are popular activities during the summer. Behind the hotel there is a large forest that is ideal for walks or horseback rides. A Finnish sauna and a nursery are also on the premises.

Rates vary from $50 (full American Plan) to $70 per day, depending on the season and room. For more information write to Mr. S. Righetti, Reservations Manager.

Excelsior Palace Hotel

30126 *Lido*
Venice
Italy

At the turn of the century the Lido became one of the world's favorite playgrounds. It was so well known that the Paris nightclub was named after it. The Excelsior Palace was one of the first hotels to be built on the Lido and it is still the center of activity for the whole beach. Although everything has been modernized to the ultimate degree, fortunately much of the original grandeur and opulence still remain.

The Palace is a big hotel. The dining rooms can feed and seat two-thousand people at a time. This is obviously not the place for those seeking quiet and solitude. The Palace is for people who like to watch the passing parade, who enjoy variety, activity and haute cuisine. All these the Palace will provide.

The hotel has its own private beach, consequently it is relatively uncrowded. A salt-water heated swimming pool has recently been built and is available if swimming in the sometimes murky waters of the Adriatic palls as a pastime.

The eighteen-hole Alberoni Golf Course is found on the western end of the island between the lagoon and the Adriatic Sea. In typically Italian fashion, even the golf course is dotted with outcroppings of old ruins, old walls and vine-covered arbors. There is a clubhouse, a bar, and a restaurant. Tennis competes with golf at this delightful spot and the four clay courts are constantly in use. A professional will help to sharpen your game, but make sure that he speaks at least a little bit of English before you start your lesson. Reservations for courts must be made a day in advance and there is a charge of approximately $3 per court per hour.

A ferry service makes commuting to Venice easy. The city's points of interest are too well known to be mentioned here, but if you are in Venice in July and August while the Biennale

Art Exhibition or the Film Festival are on, do not miss them. Remember also that the Casino is open all the year around.

For rates, contact Hotel Representative Inc., 660 Madison Avenue, New York, N.Y. 10021.

Grand Hotel
Rimini
Italy

Rimini, the famous summer resort of the Adriatic coast, with its lovely beaches, bikinis, and lively night life is the scene of much action during July and August. It is approximately sixty miles from Florence.

The Grand Hotel is an elegant oasis in the midst of all this activity. Here all is subdued, tasteful and exists only for your comfort and enjoyment. The swimming pool is the classic rectangle and after you have seen it and its landscaping, free-forms and kidney shapes seem somehow a little vulgar. Marvellous buffet luncheons are served around the pool, which is heated. A private beach, solarium, sauna, masseur and night club are the other amenities at the Grand Hotel.

There are the two clay courts at the Grand Hotel and a professional who gives lessons and makes himself very useful arranging games, finding partners and when needed, pitching in himself. Tennis has recently seen a revival in popularity here and so the spillover, if any, is welcome to use the Circolo Tennis Club, with its seven clay courts, which is just next door. The Tennis Club is a very pleasant spot with showers, a pro-shop, restaurant and bar.

This is one of Europe's old-style luxury hotels which North Americans adore because it matches their preconceived ideas of Europe as luxurious and decadent.

There are more Italians than foreign tourists here, which is a good indication of its quality. Italians are very choosy, particularly in their own country.

For information on rates write to Mr. S. Stockloew, Manager.

Hotel Cala Di Volpe

Porto Cervo
Costa Smeralda
Sardinia, Italy

Of all the resorts in this *Guide*, the Hotel Cala di Volpe is probably the must luxurious. It is a castle, half-ringed with water where every room has a private terrace and a view of the sea and mountains. Furnished with handwoven Sardinian fabrics and antiques, every room has been individually decorated. Everything is air conditioned.

Far, far away from the crowds you can swim in the olympic-size swimming pool or off one of the hotel's very private beaches. There is a harbor and jetty for mooring yachts. Fantastic restaurants, bars, boutiques, and a night club are all in the immediate vicinity.

The new eighteen-hole Pevero golf course is just next door. Designed by Robert Trent Jones, the course has extra long tees and the greens and fairways are kept green by constant use of an underground sprinkler system during the dry Sardinian summer. The sea views from the course are real spellbinders.

Tennis is played at the Cervo Tennis Club. It has four beautiful clay courts in top-notch condition, one of which is floodlit. There is a very special indoor-outdoor heated swimming pool, a restaurant where excellent lunches are served and a bar. A pro is on hand to give lessons and arrange games. Have a good look at your tennis partner — he may be an internationally known celebrity. This part of the world is popular with the jet set, particularly in August.

Loafing in the sun, horseback riding along miles of empty beaches, tennis, golf, and marvellous food and wine, are the outstanding features of this exotic corner of the world.

Not surprisingly, a holiday here is not cheap. For information on rates, write to Mr. Dieter Tzschentke, Commercial Manager, Societa Alberghiera Costa Smeralda, 07020 Port Cervo, Sardegna, Italy.

Hotel Cervo

Porto Cervo
Costa Smeralda
Sardinia
Italy

Not quite as exclusive or luxurious as the Cala di Volpe, the Hotel Cervo is nevertheless a first-class hotel. Set in the heart of Porto Cervo, it forms part of the village piazza which is the center of activity. Surrounded by cafés, restaurants, shops and boutiques, Hotel Cervo is a very lively and happy spot. Many of the rooms are cleverly designed around a gorgeous free-form swimming pool and garden. From the hotel's private creek, you can set off to cruise along the coastline or you can make use of the hotel's free shuttle service to the beach. A poolside barbecue is particularly popular with American guests. All rooms are air conditioned and have their own private terraces. The public rooms are decorated with the ornate ceramic floor tiles and heavy carved furniture that are so characteristic of Italy.

Tennis is played at the Cervo Tennis Club, previously described under *Cala di Volpe*.

The Costa Smeralda is by far the most picturesque and tourist-oriented part of Sardinia. Ideal for sailing, water skiing, or sunbathing on one of the eighty beaches in the thirty-five-mile stretch of coast, the Costa Smeralda is still relatively quiet and unspoiled.

For information concerning rates write to Mr. Dieter Tzchentke, Commercial Manager.

Regina Isabella-Sporting

Lacco Ameno
Ischia
Italy

Ischia, "the isle of eternal youth", is approximately sixteen miles from Naples to which it is connected by ferry, hydrofoil and helicopter services. A small island of roughly one-hundred

The fabulous Reid's Hotel in Madeira, Portugal, has two tennis-quick courts, and two more are available to hotel guests at the Funchal Country Club.

square miles, it has recently seen a rebirth of its tourist industry mainly because of the centuries' old thermal baths. In 1951 the baths at Lacco Ameno were restored and large hotels were built to cope with the crowds who came to be cured of a wide variety of ailments.

The Regina Isabella is a pleasant seaside hotel designed to offer many facilities and comforts. All rooms are air conditioned, terraced, and have private baths. The heated pool and the sea are so close to each other that you can swim in one or the other while using the same deck chair. All water sports are available, with water skiing being the most popular. Bowling, mini-golf, a bar with an orchestra and nightly entertainment, a hairdressing salon, and exceptionally friendly service are all to be found at the Regina Isabella.

The spa is directly connected to the hotel and is one of the best equipped I have ever seen. It has *two* thermal swimming pools, one open air and the other enclosed.

Tennis is played on two well-maintained clay courts. It is a very popular sport here with keen competition, and although there are only two courts, tournaments are regularly held for hotel guests. A professional is on hand to direct and instruct. If you want to go further afield, the town operates a tennis club in a large park by the piazza.

Ischia is a rocky, arid island. There are some interesting historical sites worth visiting. As you drive along the higher roads, wonderful views of Vesuvius and Capri unfold. The ruined Aragonese Castle of Ischia Ponte is the most important historical site on the island. Here the Normans, the Swabians, the Angevins succeeded one another and here resounded the echoes of the revolutions through which Italy won her freedom. The Shrine of St. Maria del Socconso, at Forio is another very interesting spot. While at Forio, visit the Town Hall and the Tower.

The cape and the village of St. Angelo, with the baths of Cavascura dug out in the tufa-rock, must not be missed. This is the most picturesque and primitive part of the island and cannot be reached by car. In St. Angelo Ischia still preserves her natural charm.

Very popular with Germans who seem to have more faith in the curative powers of thermal baths than any other nation, Ischia in common with the rest of the Mediterranean, is much more pleasant in the spring or fall when the hordes of tourists have either left or have not yet appeared.

For information regarding rooms, prices and special packages, write to Mr. H. Sellner, Director.

Splendido

Portofino
Italy

The Splendido is the old established hotel of the Portofino area. A large, imposing structure, it sits on a hill facing the sea and the village. Surrounded by palm trees, rose gardens, flowering shrubs and flowers, this is a very romantic spot. Flowers are everywhere — in pots, in vases, climbing on walls, and on your breakfast tray. Everything at the Splendido is done with a great deal of good taste. The opulent dining room with its air of quiet elegance, the tiled halls and lobbies furnished with antiques, and flowers in huge copper pots, the outdoor café with trailing vines, intimate views of the harbor — this is the old world at its best.

There is one newly resurfaced tennis court where many friendly games are played. There is no pro or pro-shop. For more serious tennis, plan an excursion to either St. Margherita or Rapallo, where there are active local clubs where visitors are welcome, upon payment of a small fee.

Portofino boasts a lively *bagniofore* — a beach club, to which the Splendido provides free transportation. Here you will see some of the briefest bikinis and most beautiful girls in Italy. The beach area is small and crowded, but the ambiance is good and the beach restaurant serves simple, well-prepared Italian dishes. If you do not like the hurly burly of the beach, the Splendido has its own sea-water swimming pool.

Portofino is approached by a winding coastal road with magnificent views of the sea and the mountains. The area, once only inhabited by fishermen, has now become a tourist haven.

It has many old towns, castles and churches well worth exploring.

The nearest airport is Genoa. Rapallo, about five miles away, is the nearest place for shopping, golf, art galleries and local culture.

For information on rates write to Mr. G. L. Zanotti, Manager.

PORTUGAL

Portugal is a rather melancholy country and this spirit is expressed in its sad and romantic songs called *fados*. The best way to hear this music is to visit the fado houses in the old section of Lisbon and to wander through its narrow cluttered streets.

One can drive south to the Algarve through the cork forests. The roads are bad, but staying at the government-operated *pousadas*, which are inexpensive and lovely, compensates. Faro is the airport which serves the Algarve if you want to reach the coast directly.

The Moorish influence is evident in the architecture of the south; in the vegetation — fig and almond trees; and in the physical characteristics of the people. The almond trees are glorious when they are in full bloom at the end of February, which is one of the best times to visit the Algarve, although the summer heat and the glare that reflects from the dry, white landscape are mitigated by the almost constant wind.

In addition to good shopping for leather goods, Portugal has a variety of beautiful hand-carved furnishings for the home. The Portuguese ceramic floor and wall tiles are very colorful and are beautifully designed. Their carpets have the same attributes, and the pottery is also very special. Naturally, in Madeira, one buys the incomparable lace, which can also be found in Portugal.

It is possible to dine very well in Lisbon and in other large centers, or in the occasional fine restaurant, but in general, the gastronomy is not a delight. Typical dishes are *bacalhau* (cod), *polvo* (octopus), *caldeirada* (fish soup), and grilled sardines. Desserts are good and the fruit is wonderful. Port is the national drink. Here it is less heavy than in America. White port is an excellent aperitif and *vinho verde* is a delightful accompaniment to any meal.

There are twenty-two escudos to the dollar. Portugal, once considered to be among the cheapest countries for visitors, is now on a par with the rest of Europe. This is probably due to a greater influx of tourists in recent years. A passport and vaccination certificate are required to get into Portugal.

Hotel Dona Filipa
Vale do Lobo
Almansil
Algarve, Portugal

The Algarve is still relatively undeveloped, peaceful and even backward. A few years ago, one could walk for miles along its beaches and never meet another soul. Not any more. Developments and hotels are springing up like mushrooms and land prices have skyrocketed. One of the most pleasant of these developments is the Vale do Lobo.

Owned by an English hotel chain, the Vale do Lobo, with the Hotel Dona Filipa at its center, is a well planned, efficiently run complex consisting of the 130-room Dona Filipa, a cluster of *aldeamentos* (row houses which are rented when their owners are not using them), luxurious private villas, the best golf course in the Algarve, a gorgeous stretch of clean, uncrowded beach, tennis courts, swimming pool, supermarket (where prices are high even by American standards), mini golf and a lively beach restaurant which serves good Portuguese food at international prices.

The clientele is mostly English. In fact, if you stay within the grounds of the Vale do Lobo, you will hear more English spoken than Portuguese. The hotel is tastefully, even opulently decorated. It has a very formal dining room featuring an international cuisine with endless courses. There is some live entertainment in the bar, but in general this is a quiet hotel.

The countryside is arid and scrub-like in the summer and fall. After the short winter, spring is spectacular with flowers and almond blossoms covering the whole landscape.

95

Albufeira, twenty minutes away by car, is the swinging spot of the whole area. Once an old fishing village, it now has a number of discothèques, restaurants, open-air markets and shops. La Ruina is one of the best restaurants in the Algarve. It serves delicious fish and seafood at very reasonable prices. Faro is a twenty-minute drive in the other direction, but being a new town, it is not as interesting as Albufeira.

There is no tennis pro at the Dona Filipa. The two dynaturf courts must be booked at least a day ahead and there is a small charge for their use. Playing time in the summer is limited to one hour, but you may book for several times during the day. The boy in charge of court reservations will do his best to arrange satisfactory games, but he cannot always be counted on to do this to everyone's satisfaction. There are no scheduled tournaments, clinics or round robins.

The eighteen-hole golf course is watered by an automatic watering system which means that the course is always in top shape. The clubhouse is magnificent — completely equipped with showers, changing facilities, restaurant and bar.

For more information contact Mr. Noel L. O'Neil, Manager.

Hotel Palacio
Estoril
Portugal

Portugal's playground, Estoril, is only twenty minutes away from downtown Lisbon.

The Hotel Palacio reigns supreme over Estoril. A dignified landmark for the last thirty-five years, it sits fronting the Atlantic Ocean surrounded by gardens, and cloaked in an atmosphere of old-world luxury. The rooms, furnished with eighteenth-century reproduction furniture, the crystal chandeliers, the elegant swimming pool, the gourmet meals and the attentive service are all part of a Europe which is vanishing but fortunately still exists here.

The beach is a short walk away. It is very crowded during July and August and I feel, has been greatly overrated. However, there is much life and activity on the beach, which is fun to watch. Sailing, surfing, golf are all close to the Palacio, but two of its greatest assets are right next door. These are the Casino and the Tennis Club.

The Club's seven clay courts are kept in impeccable condition and are playable the whole year around. Adam Touroc is the head professional and is available for lessons. He is fluent in English as is Olivio Silva, his assistant. Three courts are lighted at night. Many tournaments are held here every year and some are of international stature. Local tournaments to which hotel guests are invited are also a regular part of the tennis program. Playing time is limited to fifty minutes. There is a charge of $2 per person for use of the courts. Showers and changing facilities are available, as are a bar and a restaurant.

The International Gambling Casino is across the garden from the Palacio. It is open from three in the afternoon until three in the morning. Here you can try your luck playing Black Jack, roulette, craps, French bank and baccarat, or develop a sore arm working the slot machines. There is a floor show every night at 11:30. For late revelers there is another show in the Wonder Bar at 1:30 with a stripper as one of the highlights.

By night, the nooks and crannies of Cascais, just down the street from the hotel, echo to the beat of discothèques and the strum of guitars until the small hours of the morning.

The whole area around Lisbon is well worth exploring. Lisbon itself, with its cathedrals, the fishermen's Alfama district, and the fado houses, is only a short drive away. The old Portuguese cities of Sintra, Mafra, Obidos, and Evora evoke reflections of the past with their Roman ruins and bridges. Fatima is a full day's outing from Estoril.

For information on rates write to Mr. Manuel Quintas, General Manager.

Reid's Hotel

P.O. Box 401
Funchal, Madeira
Portugal

Madeira is a Portuguese island, seventy-five minutes by air away from Lisbon. It is famous for its wine industry, fisheries, and now the tourist trade. Mountainous with a semi-tropical climate, it is a wonderful place for a holiday. The weather is moderate all the year around, even in the summer when sea breezes make golf and tennis not-too-exhausting pastimes. The local wines are very good and very cheap, and also, Madeira is still off the beaten track for the hordes of tourists who descend on Europe during the summer months. In Madeira, the place to stay is Reid's.

Perched on top of a cliff a short distance from the town, Reid's offers a spectacular view of the Bay of Funchal and the Atlantic Ocean. The hotel stands in ten acres of beautifully landscaped lawns, palms and flowers. In the spring the gardens are particularly beautiful. There are 170 rooms. Most rooms face the sea (be sure to ask for one that does) and have all the modern conveniences. The cuisine can be roughly described as "international", although there is always a Portuguese section on the menu. The wine cellar has been carefully nurtured and added to over the years; it is now the best in Madeira.

During the summer, a charming garden restaurant is open for the swimmers and sunbathers at the two sea-water swimming pools. One heated pool is used even in the winter.

Some entertainment is provided, with folk dancing as the staple item but usually one is left to one's own devices. Guests are mostly English and German with a sprinkling of Americans. New Year's Eve is the big night of the year in Madeira. There are festivities galore, culminating with a spectacular display of fireworks.

Water skiing, fishing and sailing are popular. Fishing is excellent in the Bay of Funchal. A new nine-hole golf course is approximately forty-five minutes away, where Reid's guests get a special price on green fees.

There are two tennis-quick courts here; they are free to guests of the hotel and playing time is unlimited. (Tennis-quick is a surface similar to dynaturf.) An English tennis professional, Peter Gilmour and his wife run the tennis life of the hotel. Two more courts at the Funchal Country Club are also available to hotel guests. Here the tennis is more competitive, with tournaments and round robins as regular features.

Seven good all-weather tennis courts at The Hotel Atalaya Park and Country Club in Spain give tennis enthusiasts excellent daytime playing opportunities. The Club also boasts an eighteen-hole championship golf course which is possibly the best on the Costa del Sol.

The International Casino in Funchal is a major attraction. A new casino is being built, but in the meantime, there is still plenty of opportunity to pit your skills against the house.

For information on rates write to Mr. R. A. Blandy, Manager.

SPAIN

The Costa del Sol is 160 miles of coast with many fascinating excursions to be made inland to see the historic and traditional parts of Spain. For example, Ronda, in addition to being one of the oldest towns in Spain, has the oldest bullring in the country and is the home of the inimitable matador Antonio Ordonez. The town has a dramatic cliff setting, significant of its battle-torn history. The roads to Ronda from both Malaga and Marbella are appalling, but the drive through the Andalucian countryside is unforgettable.

If one has more time, both Jerez where Spanish sherry comes from, and Granada, home of the most sumptuous of all the Moorish palaces, the Alhambra, should be visited.

Southern Spain is hot and crowded in the summer and beautifully temperate most of the winter. Spring is possibly the best time to come, within two or three weeks of Easter when the *Ferias* are held. These are festive religious celebrations, full of pageantry. The most famous *Feria* is held in Seville and in Seville the most splendid hotel is the Alfonso XIII, which is an old Andalucian Palace. Naturally, one has to reserve rooms well in advance at this time of year.

Shopping in Spain is generally inexpensive, but one has to be extremely careful as the workmanship is, sadly enough, often poor. Leather goods — shoes, handbags, gloves, and suede are good buys. There is a lot of embroidery work on clothes and linen which is colorful.

Hand-painted pottery varies in design from region to region and can be very beautiful, especially the old Moorish patterns. Dolls and jewelry are other popular items.

Some of the typically Spanish dishes that the visitor should try are: *cordero asado* (baby lamb), *cochinillo* (roast pig), *jamon serrano* (mountain ham), and the more familiar exports of Spanish cuisine — *tortillas, paella* and *gazpacho*. Remember that Spaniards eat very late — lunch is any time after 1:30 and dinner is after 9:30. Everything shuts down in the afternoon for the universal *siesta*. There are approximately fifty-four pesetas to the dollar. Service is added to the bill, but a small additional tip is expected. A passport and smallpox vaccination certificate are required to get into Spain. The road from Spain to Gibraltar has been closed and to get to Gibraltar from Spain is a very complicated business.

Hotel Ancora

Tossa de Mar
Costa Brava
Spain

Tossa de Mar is a small fishing village nestled between the sea and the mountains. It is framed by medieval castles and bordered by a number of very appealing little white-sand beaches. Without a doubt it is the most picturesque and most alluring resort along the Costa Brava. Barcelona is only forty miles away.

In the middle of the village, just beside the beach, there is a small Spanish hotel which is a real gem. Built in the 1930s, it is a little oasis of tranquility and authentic Spanish cuisine. All of the forty-odd rooms have a private bath and central heating. A small grotto-like pool and one tennis court are next to the dining terrace. The tennis court is clay and is lighted for night play. A professional is available for lessons. Just a few steps away is the village beach, full of life and action.

There are many interesting coastal towns in the area waiting to be explored. The shoreline is an unusual mixture of sandy beaches and rocky promontories.

The Ancora is popular with businessmen and their families from Barcelona. It is open from April to October. The best time to come is in the spring when the area is aflame with flowers. For more information write to Mr. Jose Puig, Manager.

Tennis is played the whole year around on two tennis-quick courts at the Hotel San Felipe in the Canary Islands.

Hotel Atalaya Park and Country Club

Estepona Marbella
Costa del Sol
Spain

The Hotel Atalaya Park and Country Club is a large luxury hotel of five-hundred rooms, situated halfway between the airport at Malaga and Gibraltar. It is directly on the Mediterranean, set amidst twenty acres of tropical gardens, pools and tennis courts. This area of Spain boasts 325 days of sunshine a year and an average temperature of seventy degrees F. which makes it ideal for just about any outdoor activity with the exception of skiing and ice hockey.

The decor at the Atalaya is Spanish baronial — shining copper and brass, dark woodwork, beautifully tiled floors, heavy Spanish chairs and tables. There is even gypsy music every night after dinner.

All the latest and most modern resort luxuries are here — an enormous heated fresh-water pool with a sliding glass roof, another outdoor pool, a table d'hote dining room, beach barbecues, saunas, night club, Kontiki room, boutiques and even a fully supervised physical education program in the gymnasium.

At Atalaya, golf is played all the year around. The eighteen-hole championship golf course is reputedly the best on the Costa del Sol. A real challenge to the scratch player from the back tees, the full length is reduced by five-hundred yards for everyday players, and a further four-hundred yards for the ladies. The Clubhouse has a view of all eighteen holes, three countries and two continents.

There are seven good all-weather tennis courts at Atalaya, but no lights, the theory being that there are better things to do on the Costa del Sol after dark than to play tennis. The courts are in a picturesque setting — against a background of gnarled old olive trees and lovely views of Marbella. Denise Carter Triolo, an American who was ranked eighth in the United States in 1971, together with her husband, are the resident professionals. They both give individual and group lessons and have become very popular here. A complete pro-shop, changing and shower facilities are next to the courts.

Children have a good time at Atalaya, as there are special children's programs, a wading pool, a playground and children's meal hours.

For information on rates write to Mr. J. Duncan Newton, Manager.

Hotel Formentor

Formentor
Majorca
Spain

Formentor is a peninsula in the northeast section of Majorca. It is mountainous and remote, but has one of the most beautiful bays in the Mediterranean. The Hotel Formentor overlooks the bay, and the views, particularly from the dining terrace, are spectacular.

Open all the year around, you will get good value for your money at this hotel. Although fairly large, (131 rooms) it manages to avoid the feeling of mass production; the staff is friendly and eager to please and the other guests are very pleasant people.

There are eight tennis-quick courts, three of which are lit. Tennis-quick is a surface very similar to dynaturf. A professional runs the whole show very efficiently. Individual and group lessons, friendly games and tournaments are all arranged by him. No one, from novice to experienced player, will have any difficulty finding a good game here. Tennis is played all the year around. The summer heat is usually not oppressive because of the sea breezes from the Mediterranean.

A cosy beach with a restaurant, water skiing, fishing, sailing and horseback riding, is the center of activity during the day. A mini-golf course is very popular with both children and adults.

All rooms are air conditioned and have private bathrooms. There are two swimming pools, one of which is heated. A barber shop, beauty parlor, television room, and masseur are all on the premises, as well as a tennis pro-shop. There are no racquet restringing facilities but racquets can be rented.

Prices, with double room and all meals, vary from $15 in the off season (November to March) to $22 in the high season (March 16 to October 31).

The hotel arranges outings to historical sites, shopping trips and sightseeing tours. It is very popular with the English who come here because they know they will get lots of tennis, sun, and good food — all at a reasonable price. The Formentor's one disadvantage is that it is so far away from the mainstream of Majorca.

Hotel San Felipe

Playa de Martianez
Puerto de la Cruz
Tenerife, Canary Islands
Spain

The Canary Islands are relatively new to tourists but in recent years they have become popular among the English and Europeans because of the climate, which is mellow all the year around, and the beauty of the islands themselves.

The Hotel San Felipe is a large eighteen-story hotel built facing the beach, but across the street from it. It is just a five-minute walk away from the center of Puerto de la Cruz, an active holiday resort and seaport. The hotel is set in a tropical garden with the tennis courts, a swimming pool, and a children's wading pool all within this garden. The usual amenities of a big hotel are here — night club, restaurants, discothèque, boutiques, masseur and beauty parlor. All rooms have a view either of the sea or the mountains and are completely modern and air conditioned.

Golf and riding clubs are a thirty-minute drive away. Deep-sea fishing is very popular and very good in this area. Summer is the off season, with a corresponding lowering of prices, even though temperatures are not as high as in the south of Spain

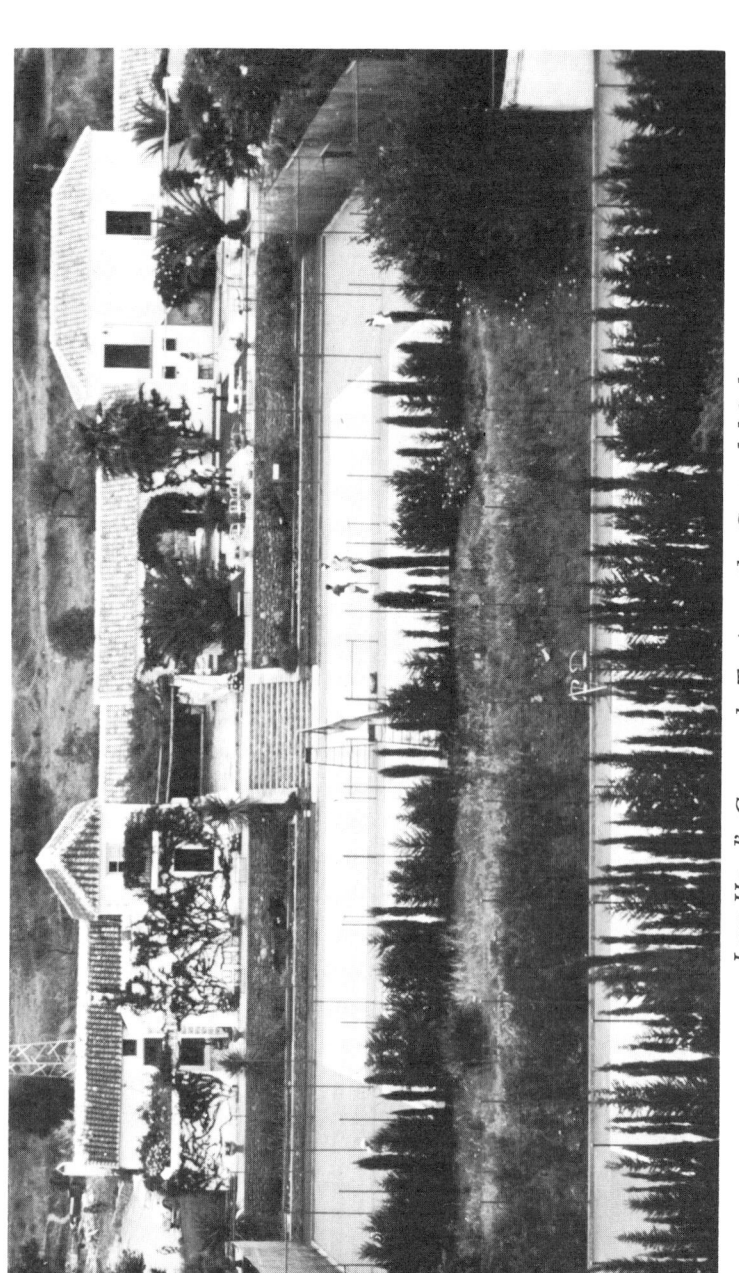

Lew Hoad's Campo de Tenis on the Costa del Sol.

or Italy, as trade winds and the Gulf Stream protect the Canaries from very hot African weather.
There are two tennis-quick courts here. This surface is fast and it dries quickly. There is a small charge for use of the courts, which have to be reserved a day in advance. Although there are only two courts, tennis is very keen here and the Hotel San Felipe is the tennis center of the area and tennis is played the whole year around. A highlight of every year is the Golden Rock Tennis Tournament when players such as Gimeno, Orantes, Gisbert and Mandarino come to play.
For guests, there are three tournaments a year. During Easter week, in October, and between Christmas and the New Year, the hotel is a hive of tennis activity. Enthusiasts come from far and wide, not only to play, but also to partake in the many social activities which are part of the tennis weeks. For information on dates and prices write to the Manager.

Lew Hoad's Campo De Tenis

Carretera de Mijas
Apartado 111
Fuengirola
Spain

Lew Hoad, one of the most famous tennis players of all time, has recently opened his Campo de Tenis on the Costa del Sol, a twenty-five minute drive from the international airport in Malaga. The Campo is really a tennis development consisting of private villas built around a central core and including five all-weather courts, a swimming pool and a clubhouse. The clubhouse facilities are very extensive. There is a bar, restaurant, sitting rooms, pro-shop, boutique, dressing rooms and showers. There is also a very pleasant outdoor sitting area from where one can enjoy being a spectator and watch the tennis matches.
As this is a very new development, it has not yet been completely finished and further plans include three more tennis courts (at present there are eight clay courts), accommodations for forty people, a sauna, gymnasium, squash courts and a putting green. Land is still available for sale. Temperatures for

playing tennis are almost ideal all the year around, except that summers can get very hot.

The Campo is within easy driving distance of many of the Costa del Sol's historic spots, such as Ronda, Cordoba, Seville, Granada and Jerez. Nearby are five championship golf courses, riding, fishing, swimming and water skiing. Marvellous small and large restaurants for all types of seafood and Spanish delicacies are everywhere.

Court rates per person per day are $5.40, per week $21.60 and per month $54. There is also a family plan: the first two people in the family pay full rates, and the remaining pay only half. The cost of a one-hour lesson from Lew Hoad is $32, from J. Beverly $16, and from G. Dudic $10. Lew's attractive wife, Jenny, conducts the children's clinics. Lew Hoad is the coach of the Spanish Davis Cup Team. Each year at the end of October the International Tennis Tournament of the Costa del Sol is held here with many of the big names participating — Manuel Santana, Manuel Orantes, Evonne Goolagong and others. For more information write to Lew Hoad at the Campo.

Many of the people who attend the Campo stay at the Hotel Las Piramides; a four-star hotel located on the beach in Fuengirola, a ten-minute drive away. The Hotel Las Piramides has 320 modern, air conditioned rooms facing the Mediterranean. The hotel itself has two courts where you can practice what you have learned at the Campo. Hotel guests do not have to pay for using these courts. The hotel has four restaurants, three very lively bars, a swimming pool and a beach.

For more information write to Mr. Jesus Diaz, Manager, Hotel Las Piramidas, Fuengirola, Costa del Sol, Spain.

Marbella Club Hotel

Marbella
Costa del Sol, Spain

The Marbella Club is one of the oldest and the most famous of all the resorts along the Costa del Sol. Small, exclusive, and expensive, it is a favorite meeting place and watering hole for members of the international set. They come here in July and

August to soak up the sun, to lounge around the pool and to enjoy the privacy of their rooms and the excellence of the Club's cuisine.

Attractive apartments and bungalows are scattered among luxuriant lawns and subtropical gardens, assuring guests a degree of privacy seldom found in a resort. Located directly on a private beach, sailing and water skiing are right here.

Although the Club has neither golf nor tennis on its premises, five championship golf courses and as many tennis clubs are within ten miles of it. Lew Hoad's Campo de Tenis, Atalaya, Los Monteros, and Sotogrande are the best of these.

The swimming pool and outdoor dining terrace have as their backdrop an unusual artificial waterfall. The view of the coastline is spectacular. At night, the pool area becomes a fairyland of candles, lanterns and brightly covered tables, when the titled, the rich and the beautiful sit down to dinner. An orchestra plays for dancing every night after dinner.

A double room with bath, without meals costs approximately $20 per day per person. A suite consisting of a double room with bath and living room costs about $30, while a bungalow with one double and one single room, two bathrooms and a living room costs $54. Full pension is about $15 per person per day extra. It is wise to reserve six months in advance, as this is the most popular and the most heavily booked hotel on the Costa del Sol. For more information write to Count Rudi Schonburg, Director General.

Los Monteros

Marbella
Costa del Sol
Spain

Los Monteros is a luxury development facing the sea, three miles from the resort town of Marbella and twenty-five miles from the airport at Malaga. It is a large complex with a predominantly English clientele. Besides the modern luxury hotel, the property also contains a number of private villas which can be rented through the hotel when not being used by their owners.

A lovely new eighteen-hole golf course, three swimming pools, a large beach with a swinging beach club (restaurant, terrace, bar, swimming pool), water sports and horseback riding are here for the amusement of the guests. All these activities and diversions are well organized, but it is the excellence of the tennis facilities that attracts many good and keen players to Los Monteros.

The Tennis Club consists of three clay and four all-weather courts, a clubhouse and a pro-shop. Two of the courts are floodlit. A staff of professionals looks after all tennis needs — they give private and group lessons, arrange games, introduce players and organize many local tournaments to which hotel guests are invited.

When there are a great many people who want to play, the courts may only be reserved for one hour a day per room and a guest may not play for longer than one hour a day. Reservations may be made the day before, after 10 p.m., and if many people want to make reservations, priority is given to those who did not play on that day. Luckily, this does not happen very often, although sometimes in July and August getting enough court time can be a problem.

Tennis is played all the year around and at the Los Monteros Tennnis Club it is taken seriously — competition is keen and the caliber of tennis is high.

The cost of accommodation varies between $40 and $80 a day for a double room with breakfast and dinner. Winter prices are slightly lower. For more information write to the Manager.

Melia Don Pepe

Finca Las Merinas
Marbella
Spain

The Don Pepe is a large, modern hotel directly on the beach, only a short walk from the downtown section of Marbella. It has three swimming pools (two of which are heated), a bridge

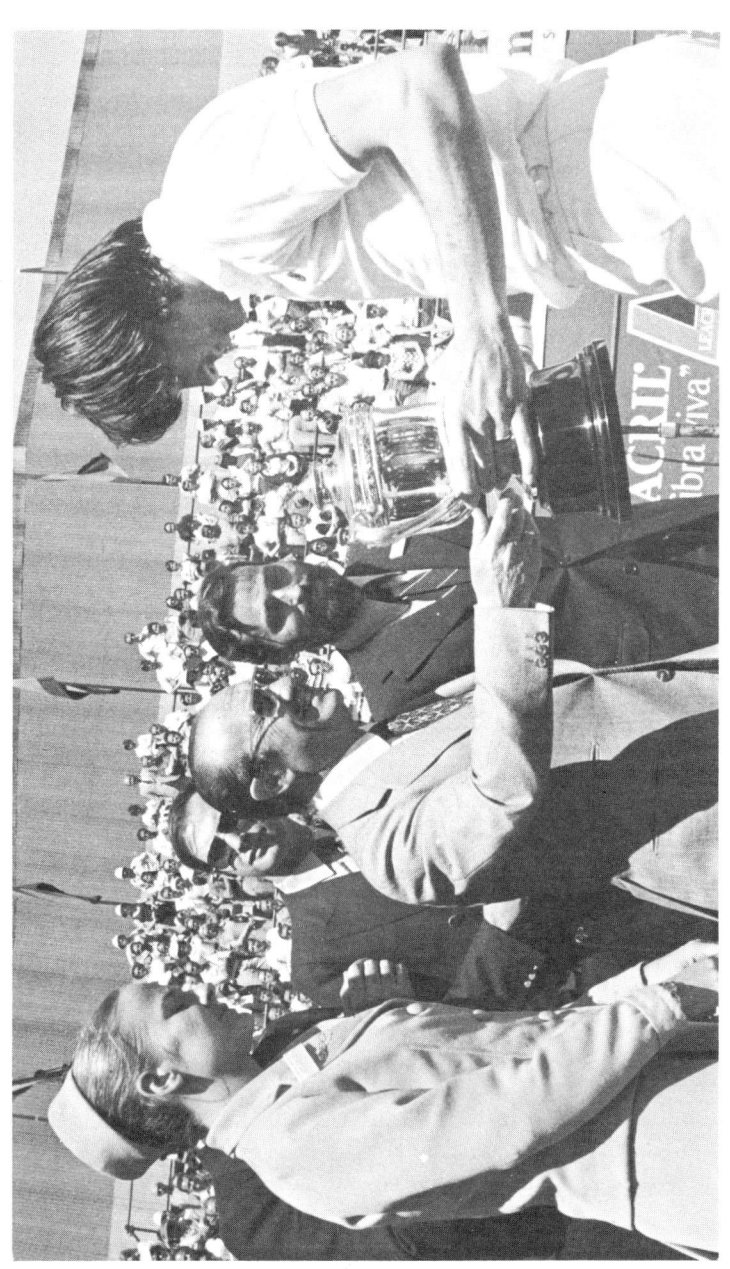

Ilie Nastase winning another trophy at the Hotel Melia Don Pepe in Spain.

club, sauna, shops and boutiques. The grill, La Farola, is famed for its gourmet fare. There is a night club, El Serrallo, which has a permanent orchestra and is open all the year around.

A large, 250-room hotel in the medium-price range, the Don Pepe is surrounded by six acres of tropical gardens. The bedrooms are all large, well furnished and each has its own terrace and bathroom.

Two eighteen-hole golf courses, the Andalucia Nueva and the Guadalmina are nearby. The guests at the Don Pepe are entitled to a twenty percent reduction on green fees at these courses. Free transportation in the hotel's twelve-seater bus is provided to and from the golf courses.

Two lighted hard-surface tennis courts are at the disposal of the guests. A professional, M. Anibal, is in attendance all the year around. The hotel also has a social director whose job it is to arrange games and friendly tournaments. These are usually held weekly. There is a charge of $1.50 per hour per court.

Marbella itself is a little town, which despite the great summer influx of tourists, still preserves an Andalucian atmosphere. With its winding, narrow streets, whitewashed fishermen's houses, open-air markets and old churches, it is fascinating to explore and to soak up a little bit of Spain, which has been largely lost in the big modern hotels.

A double room with full pension averages about $30 a day per person. For more information write to Mr. José L. Abodias, Commercial Director.

Son Vida Racquet Club

Son Vida
Palma de Mallorca
Spain

The Son Vida Racquet Club is part of a large resort development, of a type becoming more and more popular in Europe and the United States. A large area of land is subdivided into a number of lots and sold to private individuals. They, in turn, build holiday villas on the land as the developer has built a golf course, swimming pools, tennis courts and other sports

Sotogrande is one of the largest and best-equipped tennis resorts on the Costa del Sol.

amenities at the core. Usually a hotel is also a feature of these developments.

Son Vida differs from other developments in that both tennis and golf are equally important. Most of the others have beautiful golf courses with lavish clubhouses with a few tennis courts hidden in some corner. Not so at Son Vida. Here there are nine beautiful clay courts, all floodlit for night play. The courts are kept in immaculate condition and are playable the whole year around. Tournaments and friendly round robins are held every week. A heated swimming pool, a clubhouse where meals and drinks are served, a complete pro-shop featuring the latest in tennis fashions and equipment, and a full professional staff complete the tennis picture.

A round of golf and one hour of free tennis are included in the price of the rooms. Any more tennis than that and there is a small charge. Courts have to be reserved a day ahead. Playing time is limited to one hour.

There are fifty-one rooms, furnished in a Spanish decor. The public rooms have all been recently modernized and refurbished. A heated swimming pool, sauna, gymnasium and a very active riding school are also here. The hotel building was once an old castle and traces of the old atmosphere still remain.

Located less than a ten-minute drive away from Palma, and with magnificent views of both the city and the Mediterranean, Son Vida is a very good base from which to explore Majorca. For information on rates, write to Mr. Bernardo Coll, Director.

Sotogrande

Guadiaro, Cadiz
Spain

Sotogrande's 3400 acres begin at one of the Costa del Sol's finest Mediterranean beaches and its rolling grasslands and twisted cork forests continue inland toward the foothills of the Sierra Almenara Mountains. Gibraltar, only twelve miles away, looms majestically in the distance, while the Atlas Mountains in North Africa are often visible across the Straits.

Sotogrande is a sportsman's paradise. Its championship golf course, designed by Robert Trent Jones, has won worldwide acclaim. A fully automatic sprinkler system pumps out thousands of gallons of water daily to keep the Bermuda-grass fairways and greens in top condition the whole year around. Three manmade lakes add to the beauty and challenge of the eighteen-hole course. There is also a nine-hole course. Golfers are accommodated at a modern Andalucian-style clubhouse and twelve bungalows. The Club de Golf Sotogrande is a private club extending visiting privileges only to members of other recognized clubs around the world. Children under the age of fourteen are not admitted.

The Beach Club, a favorite place for sunbathers and watersports enthusiasts, is open six months of the year. Swimming, pedal boating and water skiing are the most popular activities here.

Riding is another popular recreation. Andalucian ponies can be rented for excursions over the many bridle paths throughout the property. Frequent polo matches on Sotogrande's sea-side polo ground are a novelty to North American guests. A small bullring is the scene of "tientas", where one can try one's hand at fighting wild calves.

The Sotogrande Tennis Club, located in the middle of the property, provides accommodation for the whole family. Its forty double bedrooms each have their own private bath and patio. The hotel is fully air conditioned and its facilities include a restaurant, cocktail and poolside bars, card and billiard rooms, an outdoor swimming pool and a wading pool in the children's playground area. A "belle epoque" discothéque livens the night hours. A row of shops adjacent to the hotel includes men's and women's hairdressers, a boutique, an art gallery and a travel agency. A free microbus service connects the Tennis Club to the beach.

There are six all-weather tennis courts, a fully qualified professional staff and complete restringing and rental facilities. Tennis is, of course, played the whole year around. The most crowded months are July and August, but except during these months, getting enough playing time is never a problem and playing time is unlimited. There is no charge for use of the courts to guests of the hotel.

Players in 'The Golden Rock' tennis tournament at the Hotel San Felipe in the Canary Islands.

The closest international airport is in Malaga, sixty-five miles away. The countryside is full of small white villages and, in the spring, brilliant fields of flowers. The local people are pleasant and hospitable and one does not sense the attitude of indifference that is so widespread today in France.

For information on rates, write to Mr. Emilio Mena, Subdirector, Sotogrande Tennis Hotel.

SWITZERLAND

Everything in this country runs as well as a good Swiss watch. Since 1848, Switzerland has maintained both its neutrality and a stable government. Although there are four official languages — French, German, Italian and Romansh, being understood is never a problem.

The scenery is majestic at all times of year, and one shouldn't miss driving through the Alpine parts of the country. The flowers in the high meadows are lovely in the summer and combined with the gaily painted houses, they make a medley of bright colors. The remote and serene lake country also has its charm.

Zurich is the commercial center of the country. It is an attractive city, with its lake and river. The shopping is excellent. Naturally, clocks and watches are good buys. Leather and cotton goods (particularly blouses) are also reasonable in cost.

Swiss food is as mixed as its cultures. Desserts are excellent; there is a wide variety of cheeses and the chocolate is beyond compare. The local wine (offenen wein) is normally very good and the beer is excellent. Service in restaurants and hotels is efficient and polite.

There are approximately twenty-nine Swiss francs to the dollar.

Dolder Grand Hotel

8032 *Zurich*
Switzerland

Situated in a quiet residential section of Zurich and overlooking the city, is an excellent spot where one can play tennis and relax between planes. The Dolder is a spacious two-hundred-room hotel, surrounded by woodlands, gardens, a golf course and tennis courts. A car service to downtown Zurich, about five miles away, is provided by the hotel.

There are five hard tennis courts on the hotel property. They are all lighted for night play. These courts are the home of the Zurich Tennis Club, but hotel guests get priority for their use. A professional is on hand. He charges $8 for a forty-minute lesson. There is a charge of $1.50 per person per hour for use of the courts. The tennis season is from April to November.

There is also a nine-hole golf course as well as a swimming pool within the hotel grounds. A unique feature of the pool is its artificial waves.

The hotel is open all the year around and is run with the efficiency and good service for which the Swiss are so famous. The food here is good and abundant. Sunday lunch features an enormous smorgasbord which draws gourmands from all over Zurich.

For information on rates write to Mr. Georges C. A. Hangartner, Manager.

Palace Hotel
Gstaad
Switzerland

Gstaad is located in the western region of the Bernese Oberland, 3610 feet above sea level. It can be easily reached from Lausanne, Geneva and Zurich. In the summer the village is a haven of peace and quiet with lovely Alpine scenery, four cable ways ascending to 9850 feet and many sports activities.

Summer glacier skiing, mountain climbing, trout fishing, riding, and, of course, tennis are all well organized and very popular. A scenic nine-hole golf course is on the outskirts of the village. The summer season lasts from May to October.

The Palace Hotel is a gracious and relaxing place for a holiday. The food, service and quality of accommodation are all top notch.

There are four clay courts at the hotel and eight more in the village, a short walk away. The village courts are the scene of the Swiss International Open Tournament, which is held in July. Many of the big names enter and the village throbs with life during the week of this tournament. There is no charge for use of the courts at the Palace, but reservations must be made at least a day in advance. However, getting enough court time is not a problem, as the village courts are so near. Jacques Hermenjat, a well known Swiss professional, runs a sports shop and gives lessons. Lessons cost $9 for forty minutes of instruction.

The hotel has a large inodor-outdoor pool with its own snack bar and changing facilities. A bar and the most popular discothèque in Gstaad are in the cellar.

For information on rates write to Mr. Roland Abisetti, Manager.

A tournament in progress on the center court in Gstaad, Switzerland. There are four clay courts at the Palace Hotel, and eight more in the village.

CHAPTER 6
MEXICO

Before going to Acapulco, every visitor to Mexico should first stop in Mexico City. The Reforma Inter-Continental, the Maria Isabel, Camino Real and the El Presidente are first-class hotels in the Pink Zone. This area has the most exclusive shops and restaurants and is near many places of interest, such as the Museum of Anthropology, the Palace of Maximilian and Carlotta, Diego Rivera's murals and interesting residential areas. Architecture in Mexico City is visually very exciting and their use of natural, locally found building materials is a pleasing characteristic everywhere in Mexico.

The shopping in Mexico City is outstanding. There is an endless variety of beautiful things for sale — antiques, objets d'art, clothes, jewelry, silver and gold, pottery and native handicrafts. The whole city teems with excitement and gaiety.

Acapulco, a forty-minute plane ride away, also teems with gaiety and excitement. Its beaches are crowded with restaurants, tourists, peddlers, and strolling musicians who will even sell their instruments if you show an interest in them. The shops are full of lovely articles, but prices are higher than in Mexico City.

The pace is very relaxed. Lunch is never before 2 o'clock or dinner before 10 o'clock. Margaritas (tequila, lime juice and salt) and banana daquiris are the favorite drinks. Wine, gin, and scotch are very expensive all over Mexico.

The sunsets and views of the Bay are spectacular. *Turista* is not as prevalent as in years gone by, but take a supply of Enterovioform along just in case it strikes. Avoid drinking tap water, eating salads and never eat in roadside stands. From December to May, the weather in Acapulco can be depended on one hunderd percent.

In Acapulco, people dress as nowhere else — there is an Acapulco style which one notices immediately. The rule is that anything and everything goes, as long as it is colorful and different. To get into Mexico, one needs a Mexican tourist card, which is obtainable either through a travel agent or from Mexican Tourist Boards upon presentation of a passport or birth certificate. A smallpox vaccination is no longer required. There are 12.50 pesos to the dollar. A tip of fifteen percent of the total bill is customary in all restaurants.

Acapulco Princess

Aptdo. Postal 1351
Acapulco Gro.
Mexico 4-31-00

 The Princess must be seen to be believed. Built at vast expense, it is a monument to what money and imagination can produce. Located on the new "gold coast", the Princess is halfway between Acapulco and the airport, approximately six miles away from downtown Acapulco. It faces a magnificent sweep of beach and is surrounded by lush fairways, gardens, pools and waterfalls. The main building is built in the form of an Aztec pyramid. The lobby is enormous with a glass ceiling especially designed so that both moonlight and sunlight can shine on the brightly dressed throngs far below.
 A vast hotel of eight-hundred rooms, it offers every possible luxury and convenience that you have ever dreamt of, along with a few you didn't even know existed. A purple waterfall cascading over a cocktail bar falls in the latter category. The entertainment, the shopping, and the dining areas are so many and so varied that one does not have to leave the hotel to be constantly diverted and amused.
 The 1500-foot beach is the center of the action during the day. It is a mecca for local peddlers who sell silver and gold jewelry, embroidered linens, puppets, blankets, straw products of every size and description, bikinis, and a host of other unlikely goods right on the beach. Bargaining is the order of the day.
 Sports facilities at the Princess cannnot be matched anywhere

else in Acapulco. There are two salt-water lagoon pools and a fresh-water pool featuring underground music. There is horseback riding and all the water sports, including deep-sea fishing and parasailing. Thirty-six holes of tournament-caliber golf on two of Mexico's great courses surround the Princess. The clubhouse has a pro-shop, a practice fairway and a putting green. Green fees are $8 for eighteen holes; carts cost $10.

Tennis is played under ideal conditions. There are four dynaturf outdoor courts, as well as two air conditioned indoor courts. These are the ultimate in surfacing, lighting and temperature control. The outdoor courts are also lighted.

Bill Sweeney is the head pro. A half-hour lesson from him costs $16. A lesson from the assistant pro costs only $8. Prices, for use of the courts are high — $12 an hour for the air conditioned courts day or night, and $3.20 an hour for the outdoor courts, without lights. To play outdoors with lights costs $6.80 an hour extra. The courts are open to visitors who have to pay considerably more than hotel guests. They must be reserved a day ahead of time. Playing time is limited to one hour. If you can afford them, the air conditioned courts are fabulous, as the heat of Acapulco can be oppressive to those unused to it. All equipment can be rented. There is a complete pro-shop, which does restringing.

For Modified American Plan, rates start at $34 double occupancy per person and go as high as $63. Summer rates are considerably lower. There are special honeymoon plans and holiday packages. For more information write to Ms. Connie Flores, Reservations Manager.

Pierre Marques Hotel and Golf Club

Acapulco
Mexico

If you want to go to Acapulco, but don't want to be part of its carnival atmosphere, the Pierre Marques Hotel and Golf Club is the ideal spot for you. Located equidistantly from the airport and Acapulco, (approximately five miles), the Pierre Marques is a modern hotel, tastefully planned, and built on a big, beautiful beach. The beach and the surf are both spectacular, but one must be careful here of the undertow. The grounds are beautifully landscaped, with tall coconut palms, lawns, and a golf course surrounding the hotel.

A large kidney-shaped pool overlooking the sea is a popular place for lunch and lazing.

There are five lighted, all-weather tennis courts here. During the winter season, which is the sensible time to play tennis in Acapulco, Jorge Solana is the head pro. A half-hour lesson from him costs $16 U.S.; a half-hour lesson from the assistant pro costs only $8 U.S. Special clinics and friendly tournaments are arranged when there is a demand for them. Ball boys are on duty to chase balls. This is not such a luxury as it sounds — Acapulco is hot. Nobody plays tennis between twelve and four o'clock and even in the cooler hours, chasing balls isn't much fun.

Court costs: day time — winter $3.20 U.S. per hour per court; summer $2.00 U.S. Playing with lights in the winter costs $6.80 U.S. per hour per court; in the summer $4 U.S.

Mexico's best golf architect, Percy Clifford, designed the golf course. The course, eighteen holes, par 72, is built around the hotel. Eight man-made lakes add to its challenge. A round clubhouse, well equipped for both golf and tennis has showers, a bar and a snack restaurant.

There are two-hundred air-conditioned rooms and bungalows, each with its own terrace and ocean view. The hotel has a beauty parlor, barber shop, sauna, dress shop, gift shop, drug store, jeep rental, travel service and complete valet service on its premises. Variety acts, bands, and strolling guitarists entertain until the small hours of the morning. The Princess, with its even more lavish entertainment program, is just a short walk down the beach.

Acapulco is not far away. Don't miss the diving exhibitions, or the bullfights. A pelota (jai alai) match is an exciting experience.

For information on rates, write to Mr. Rudi Hasenauer, General Manager.

Tres Vidas En La Playa
Acapulco
Mexico

Tres Vidas is a new resort about a half-hour drive away from downtown Acapulco. The builders of Tres Vidas claim that Acapulco itself is too much like Miami Beach to be really chic. Consequently they have built Tres Vidas in a very quiet spot on the Pacific Ocean on the other side of the airport from Acapulco. Conceived and established as a private playground for royalty, the worlds of government, finance and society, Tres Vidas is the very last word in luxury, beauty and sports facilities.

Here, amid four-hundred acres of tropical opulence you can sharpen your skills at golf, tennis, skeet shooting, fishing and hunting for wild boar. An olympic-size swimming pool, sailing on a large freshwater lake, deep-sea fishing, scuba diving, horseback riding and a beautiful white-sand beach (with a big surf) are all at your fingertips.

The private accommodations and public rooms are superb; the main clubhouse looks like an old hacienda, a conglomeration of patios clustered together. The use of carved wood, stone, hand-made brick, and other locally found natural materials is visually very exciting. A health spa is also on the premises.

Directing Tres Vidas tennis activity is none other than the great Don Budge. Thirteen courts (clay, grass and composition) are illuminated for use in the evenings. Coaches, ball boys, a fully equipped pro-shop with restringing facilities, a clubhouse and a bar, all help to make Tres Vidas one of the great tennis resorts. Members of Tres Vidas pay no court fees at any time, but guests staying at the Club pay:

$2.00 per person per hour for daytime hard courts
$3.00 per person per hour for grass courts
$4.00 per person per hour for night courts

All fees are based on doubles play. For singles, the fees are fifty percent higher; however doubles take precedence over singles. In the event that all courts are booked, those wishing to play singles must either double up with two waiting players, or pay twice the applicable fee. Play is limited to one hour if there are people waiting. Reservations may be made up to twenty-four hours in advance. When reserving courts, members of Tres Vidas have preference. Tres Vidas also operates a children's tennis camp during July and August. Daily rates for members, European Plan, range from $45 for one bedroom to $240 for a four-bedroom villa. Each villa has a private swimming pool. For members' guests, a $15 per day room charge is added.

For additional information contact the U.S. office at 311 South Akard, Dallas, Texas 75202, telephone (214)747-7741.

Villa Vera

P.O. Box 560-488
Acapulco
Mexico

Set against a background of tropical greenery, the Villa Vera sits perched on a hill overlooking beautiful Acapulco Bay. It is an easy walk to the main boulevard, with its shops, beaches and big hotels, but the Villa Vera itself is a haven of beauty and gaiety. Every afternoon Acapulco's jet setters gather here and the action around the pool has to be seen to be believed.

The food is excellent and is served in a dining area around the swimming pool. There is a variety of accommodations, ranging from rooms overlooking the tennis courts to luxurious bungalows with their own pools. There are in all, accommodations for a hundred and twenty people.

There are three clay tennis courts. The courts are lighted for night play. Outside visitors pay $3 per person per hour for use of the courts. Hotel guests do not have to pay for use of the courts. Ball boys are $1.60 per court per hour and lights cost $4.80 per hour. Lessons from the pro are $8 for half an hour. There is no pro-shop. Courts have to be reserved at least a day ahead. There are no round robins or tournaments, but the boy who takes reservations tries to arrange compatible games. The courts are kept in superb condition and tennis here is very keen, despite the heat of Acapulco.

In season, a double room, Modified American Plan costs $53.50, off season only $20.80. A cottage with a private pool costs $100 a day in the winter and only $40 from April 15 to November 30. During the off season there are also special honeymoon and package deals. For more information contact Mr. Wolfgang Harbich, General Manager.

Ilie Nastase, the 1972 U.S. singles champion, at the Pierre Marques Hotel and Golf Club in Acapulco, Mexico.

John Gardiner's Tennis Ranch in Scottsdale, Arizona combines good living with keen tennis, and offers some of the best weekly tennis clinics in North America.

CHAPTER 7
THE UNITED STATES

According to an estimate compiled by the A. C. Nielsen Company for the United States Lawn Tennis Association, there were ten million tennis players in 1970 in the United States, and by 1975 there will be twelve million. An increase in leisure time and a growing awareness of the importance of keeping physically fit are presumably the key factors in the growing popularity of the game.

The great tennis states are California and Florida. Their climate, their many holiday resorts, and their outdoor life style are responsible for the popularity of tennis in these two states.

In Florida, the average winter temperature is sixty-eight degrees F. but the temperature range can be wide, and cold snaps are not uncommon. In the winter, the sea off northern Florida is too cold for swimming. During the summer, temperatures are moderated by sea breezes and the heat is generally not overpowering.

Sports are an important part of life in Florida — both the spectator and participation varieties. Horse racing, jai alai, football, dog racing, golf, tennis, fishing and water sports are among the most popular.

There are many things to do. See the Everglades and watch the alligator wrestlers, visit Hemingway's house in Key West and the Kennedy Space Center in Cape Canaveral, join the masses in Disney World. If money is no object, go to at least one of the lavish big-name floor shows in Miami Beach.

Frogs legs, grits, hearts of palm salad, and oranges fresh off the trees are the culinary highlights. In Miami there are some very good Cuban restaurants and the big hotels in Miami Beach serve excellent kosher food. The Coconut Grove area of Miami has the best eating places in all of Florida.

The western coast resorts appeal mainly to the elderly. This is also true of Miami Beach, Florida, in spite of hordes of tourists, has remained a very friendly place.

In Southern California the winters are cool and relatively smogless; the summers are warm and hazy. In the north, winters are wet and windy; summers on the coast are cool, but the interior is like an oven.

There are many interesting places to see in California. Disneyland, William Randolph Hearst's castle, movie and television studios in Hollywood, homes of the stars, forests, mountains, deserts; they are all part of the strange mixture that is California. A drive along the coastal highway is a scenically unforgettable experience.

California runs the gamut in restaurants, from fast-food outlets to the most elegant in wining and dining. It is also one place where one is never embarrassed to order the local wine. In fact, it is considered almost rude not to. The prices are reasonable ($3 to $3.50 for a liter of Burgundy or Chablis) and the wines are good.

John Gardiner's Tennis Ranch

5700 *East McDonald Drive*
Scottsdale
Arizona 85253

John Gardiner's Tennis Ranch on Camelback Mountain in Arizona's Paradise Valley is a total tennis experience. If all the tennis you can play, super-luxurious accommodations, and the finest in food and wine are your idea of bliss, here it is. Basically, Gardiner's tennis resort means plush living and luxurious wining and dining sandwiched in between thousands of forehands, backhands, serves, volleys and overheads.

Clinics are structured according to ability, and one finds every degree of proficiency here. Each clinic of twenty students has six professionals and lasts for roughly three-and-a-half hours a day. At the Ranch there are fifteen all-weather (plexipave) tennis courts and the most modern teaching aids and equipment in the world. The Gardiner system includes ball machines (three-thousand balls an hour), a closed-circuit television system for instant replay, and tennis strategy lessons which are given with the aid of a tennis-court table to demonstrate proper court positioning. Tournaments are held every Saturday. The minimum age for participation in clinics is eighteen.

You do not *have* to join a clinic. Many people don't, and have a lot of fun playing among themselves. Court time is almost never a problem and nobody leaves the Ranch feeling that they did not play enough tennis. In all, there are twelve pros; a private lesson costs $18 per hour, but there is no charge for use of the courts. All tournaments are incorporated within the clinic programs. The Ranch is popular with a well-heeled over-thirty crowd who are keen tennis players and who can afford the steep prices.

A massage therapist is on hand to assuage tired and aching muscles and a yoga instructor teaches how to increase concentration. Other attractions include three swimming pools, a number of nearby golf courses, horse and dog races in Phoenix, riding stables and the shopping areas of Phoenix and Scottsdale. The famous 5th Avenue shopping area is only a five-minute drive away.

Accommodation is in forty, two-bedroom luxury condominiums, called casitas. Each casita has a living room with fireplace and completely equipped kitchen. A double room with all meals and tennis clinic averages $575 per session, per person. Tennis clinics are held weekly, from October to the end of May. For more specific information on rates and special packages write to Mr. Raymond T. Farrow, Manager. The telephone number is 602-948-2100.

Marriott's Camelback Inn

P.O. Box 70
Scottsdale
Arizona

Marriott's Camelback Inn is just twenty minutes away from Phoenix Sky Harbor Airport but it seems worlds away. Here, within its secluded sixty-five acres, is another world of luxury, seclusion, and comfort. The architecture of the main lodge and

Tennis is a popular year-round sport at Marriott's Camelback Inn in Arizona. Bright arc lights make it possible to enjoy a good game or lesson well into the evening.

the 285 rooms is a striking blend of modern and Pueblo, and the swimming pools, tennis courts, cactus gardens and golf course have all been beautifully designed around it.

The eighteen-hole, 6687-yard golf course is well known as one of the most challenging in the area. Horseback riding, taking the cure at the health spa, and shopping in Scottsdale are favorite occupations of the guests. The food at the Camelback Inn is uniformly excellent. It is a blend of western and international, plus many local specialties such as home-baked bread and outdoor steak fries. Many Hollywood celebrities come to Camelback to play tennis and to enjoy its cuisine.

There are six all-weather tennis courts, all with lights for night play. The pro is Rick Hlava, a well known tennis personality in the area. A pro-shop is on the premises where rental equipment is available and racquet restringing is done. During the Thanksgiving, Christmas and Easter holidays many friendly tournaments and special clinics are staged. In the busy seasons, courts must be reserved ahead of time, at a cost of $1.50 per person per hour. A private lesson costs $15 per hour. There is an excellent junior program here during school vacation periods.

The cost of a holiday at the Camelback Inn can vary greatly, depending on the season and type of accommodation. Prices start at $25 per double room, European Plan in the off season (the summer months) and go up to $125 a day for a suite in the high season. For more information write to Ms. Phyllis Thompson, Reservations Manager. The telephone number is 602-948-1700.

Racquet Club Ranch

Tucson
Arizona

Opened only recently, the Racquet Club Ranch is one of the largest tennis resorts in the United States, and judging from its many satisfied guests, a great success. It is located on the outskirts of Tucson and is easily accessible either by air or road.

There are thirty-four laykold tennis courts and forty-four guest casitas as well as hotel accommodations. Ideally situated in the foothills of the Catalina Mountains, The Racquet Club guarantees nearly perfect weather for tennis all the year around, with the exception of July, August and September which are very hot.

It also offers and guarantees to all of its guests, regardless of their playing level, a game at any time. The Club has a local membership of nearly four hundred from the Tucson area. "Most resorts make it impossible to get a good game unless you bring it with you," says Joe Tofe, the head of the Club. "Here a guest can play with ten different players at his skill level and meet a lot of people. He can come as a single and play every day, or come as a doubles team and find all the tennis activity he could hope for."

There is a teaching staff of sixteen pros; Margaret Court, Jim Reffkin and Craig Hardy are among them. A private lesson costs $15 per hour; a group lesson for four people $16 per hour. There are many special tennis clinics and tournaments throughout the year and, of course, there is a large pro-shop which does restringing.

In addition to tennis, the Racquet Club has an olympic-size swimming pool and a health club with sauna. Horseback riding with miles of trails around the club is also a popular activity.

Rates vary according to season and quality of accommodation. Prices range from $27 a day for a two-bedroom apartment from May to September, to $65 a day for a three-bedroom house in the winter season. All apartment units include kitchens. There are also full hotel accommodations and special tennis packages. For more information write to Mr. Joe Tofe, Manager.

The Beverly Hills Hotel

9641 *Sunset Boulevard*
Beverly Hills
California

If you are planning a business trip to Los Angeles, bring your tennis racquet and stay at the Beverly Hills Hotel.

The Sand and Beach Club, located on the premises, has two championship tennis courts run exclusively for hotel guests.

Alex Olmedo, a well known name in tennis, is the pro. He gives lessons and arranges compatible games.

Other facilities include an olympic-size swimming pool, private cabanas and white sand for sunbathers.

For information on rates write to Mr. Mal Sibley at The Beverly Hills Hotel.

Del Monte Lodge

On the Seventeen Mile Drive
Pebble Beach, California 93953

The Pebble Beach area has been described as the greatest meeting place of land and sports and sea in existence, and the Del Monte Lodge does not dispel this rumor. Scenically breathtaking, the Del Monte Lodge strives for, and to a large extent achieves, the atmosphere of an old-world inn or exclusive country club. Set on the southern edge of Del Monte Forest, a reserve of five-thousand acres, the Lodge looks out to Carmel Bay and the Santa Lucia Mountains. Both the food and the wine cellar are first rate.

Tennis is played at the Beach and Tennis Club, which is a private club, but guests of the Lodge have playing privileges. A pro-shop, showers, bar and restaurant are within the Club complex. There is a charge of $3 per one-and-a-half hour playing period. The professional is Don Hamilton, a well known tennis name in the area. Lessons cost $8.50 per hour. Del Monte Lodge has a long history of tennis enthusiasm — the first Davis Cup matches were played here. Today, there are eleven plexipave courts. They do not have lights. Courts must be reserved the day before you want to play.

Six championship golf courses are nearby, including the famous Pebble Beach. Other activities include swimming in the heated pool, horseback riding, and browsing through the beautiful and interesting Monterey area.

Prices start at $39 per day Modified American plan. For more information write to the Manager.

La Costa Resort Hotel and Spa
Costa del Mar Road
Rancho La Costa
California 92008

A large, sprawling luxury resort complex and spa, La Costa is a thirty-minute drive from San Diego and ninety minutes away from Los Angeles. It offers a wide choice of accommodations, ranging from large studio rooms to three-bedroom villas and luxury executive homes.

Tennis is a very popular sport at La Costa. There are seventeen all-weather lighted courts, with an additional eighteen being built. Each court is individually fenced and screened. The head professional is Pancho Segura. The assistant pros are Art Tilten, Pat Todd and Nels Peterson and there is a tennis hostess, Roxie Turpin, who arranges tournaments and matches players. Lessons at La Costa are not cheap — $30 for a one-hour private lesson and $60 for an hour's lesson for a group of six. Hotel guests do not have to pay for use of the courts and getting enough court time is never a problem here.

Tennis lessons feature a closed-circuit video-tape system with instant replay. There is also a practice court with an automatic ball service. A complete pro-shop with same-day restringing facilities is within the tennis complex, as are a bar and restaurant.

The climate at La Costa is ideal for outdoor sports all the year around, rarely varying by more than ten degrees. Besides tennis, there is the famous La Costa championship golf course, site of the PGA Tournament of Champions. The Saddle Club with good saddle horses and twenty-one miles of riding trails, The Beach Club on a broad, clean sand beach and excellent deep-sea fishing are the other activities here.

The health spa is simply fantastic. Nowhere else will you find a spa like La Costa's. There are saunas, rocksteam baths, herbal wraps, mineral whirlpool baths, medicinal waters and Roman baths, to mention just a few.

A favorite spot for show business personalities, who come

The Racquet Club Ranch in Tucson, Arizona has nineteen plexipave tennis courts and special tennis packages available to guests.

here to relax and to stay in shape, at La Costa the guests are really pampered.

Depending on the season, rates for double-occupancy rooms vary from $38 to $57, European Plan.

For more information write to the Reservations Manager.

Murrieta Hot Springs

Murrieta
California 92362

World famous for its natural hot mineral and tule mud baths since 1902, Murrieta Hot Springs Spa, eighty-five miles south of Los Angeles, has in recent years been completely refurbished, modernized and expanded. There are now special dietary dining rooms and bars, facial treatment and make-up rooms, sun decks, saunas, gyms, an outdoor swimming pool, tennis courts, exercise classes, massage, hydro-therapy pools and a new Robert Trent Jones eighteen-hole championship golf course.

There are eight all-weather tennis courts, with two more in the planning stages. All are lighted for night play. Two days a week free tennis clinics and group lessons are held for spa guests, as well as special junior clinics during school vacation periods. Private lessons are also available at $10 per hour from the resident pro Ed Walker, who has played with such greats as Bobby Riggs, Ted Schroeder and Jack Kramer. Roy Emerson is the touring pro. Tournaments for guests are a regular feature of the tennis program at Murietta. Hotel guests do not pay for the use of the courts. Getting enough court time is almost never a problem here.

Some of the top names in tennis have played in tournaments and have stayed at Murrieta — Charlton Heston, Richard Crenna, Gary Crosby, Doug McClure, Abby Dalton, Macdonald Carey, Ed Ames, Sam Match, Bobby Riggs, Tony Trabert, to mention just a few.

The spa program maintains a staff of fifty-six, each an expert in his particular field, whether facial rejuvenation, diet, or exercise.

Rates are approximately $65 a night for two people, including breakfast and dinner. For more specific information write to Mr. Bill Peirce, Manager.

Silverado
1600 *Atlas Peak Road*
Napa, California 94588

Silverado, which was once a historic estate, is now a very pleasant resort in the heart of the Napa Valley a fifty-minute drive north from San Francisco. Accommodating 250 people in cottages built around the original mansion, it has eight plexipave tennis courts, ball-return equipment, a complete pro-shop and tennis professional Tom Stow who gives private lessons for $20 an hour. There are no regular guest tournaments or clinics, but racquet restringing is done on the premises and the courts have lights. A charge of $2.00 per person per hour on weekdays and $3.00 on weekends is levied for use of the courts. The climate is mild and tennis can be played the whole year around.

Silverado has two championship golf courses and the Kaiser International Golf Tournament is played here. Four swimming pools, horseback riding, and a well organized children's program contribute to make Silverado a good vacation bet. Exploring the many historic sites of the area is another popular pastime.

The food here is uniformly of high quality, with a spectacular weekly buffet the culinary highlight. As this area is the center of America's wine industry, tasting and savoring vintages is a favorite occupation. Presently under construction are holiday homes and villas surrounding the golf courses, which will be rented when their owners are not using them.

For information on rates write to Ms. Sharon Woolworth at Silverado.

The Broadmoor
Colorado Springs
Colorado 80901

Exuding an atmosphere of Edwardian opulence, The Broadmoor is unique both in terms of its size and the variety of

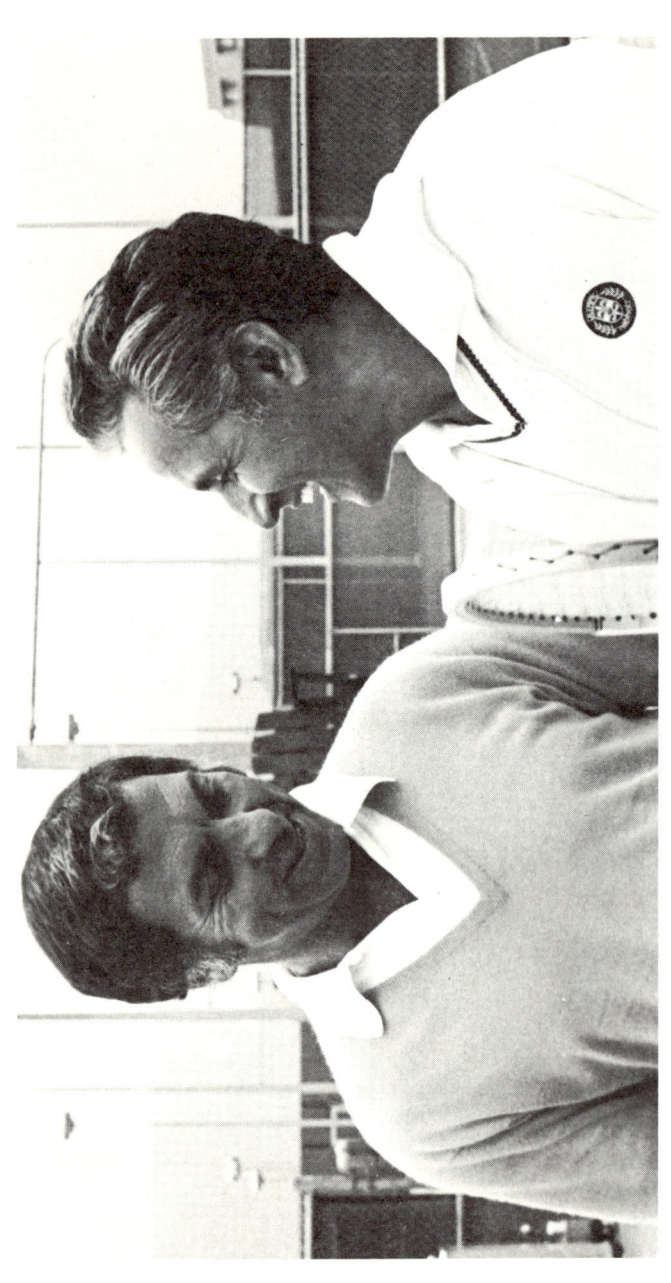

Mr. Merv Adelson, President of the La Costa Resort Hotel in California, and Pancho Segura, the resident tennis professional. There are currently seventeen all-weather lighted courts, with an additional eighteen being built.

sports, entertainments and activities it has to offer. It was opened in 1918 and has been expanding ever since. It is now a very popular convention hotel. Here is a list of just some of its attractions: two championship eighteen-hole golf courses, two swimming pools (one heated and glass enclosed), a private lake, squash, handball, a 155-stall riding arena, skiing, trap shooting, curling, water skiing, fishing, and a remarkable climate — sunny, dry and temperate all the year around.

There are six all-weather tennis courts, two of which are covered by a bubble during the winter months. The courts do not have lights. The pro is Chet Murphy, who together with an asistant, runs the tennis show. The Annual Broadmoor Invitation Tennis Tournament is held here in August. It is recognized by the USLTA for ranking purposes. There is a charge of $5 per court per hour in the summer, and $8 per hour for use of the bubble. Good children's tennis clinics are held during July and August, as well as a number of friendly tournaments. A pro-shop, snack bar, showers and changing rooms complete the tennis picture.

The price of rooms varies from $30 to $40 per day during July and August, which is the height of the summer season. This does not include meals. For more information, write to the Reservations Manager.

The Timbers —
The Cliff Buchholz Tennis Resort
P.O. Box 1033
Steamboat Springs
Colorado 80477

The Cliff Buchholz Tennis Resort at the Timbers in the Colorado mountains, offers both a get-away-from-it-all vacation and an opportunity to improve one's tennis game. Here is tennis coaching and individualized instruction at its best. Nine instructors, combined with eleven all-weather courts, video-tape playback for instantaneous coaching and study, ball-throwing machines, an indoor training center with mirrors, classrooms, special tennis alleys, and an exercise room, will all do wonders for your game.

There are at least four hours of tennis training every day, but most people start early and play late. The tennis section is only one facet of the Timbers, a well-designed vacation complex six miles southeast of Steamboat Springs. Besides tennis, there is horseback riding, fishing, and a mineral-spring pool. A good western-style cuisine is another asset.

$325 for a one-week session includes room (double occupancy), meals, all instruction and all planned activities. There are also children's sessions for $550 per three-week session. Open from May until October, the Timbers is an ideal family resort and many of the same families come back year after year. For more information, write to Cliff Buchholz at the Timbers.

The Washington Hilton
1919 Connecticut Avenue
Washington, D.C. 20009

You can mix your business with pleasure at this active in-town resort. A large hotel of twelve-hundred rooms and numerous meeting and function rooms, the Washington Hilton has on its premises a well run Racquet Club consisting of three excellent har-tru courts. While most of the elite of Washington are members, the Club is automatically open to hotel guests. The courts are playable from April 1 to the end of November. They are available on a reservation basis at $2 per hour per court on weekdays, and $4 per hour per court on the weekends. The resident pro is Donald Floyd. Private lessons are available to hotel guests. The Club helps guests find partners and arranges games.

After tennis, you can cool off in the huge swimming pool and have a meal in the outdoor garden restaurant. For tennis players, the Washington Hilton is *the* place to be. Room rates should be obtained through the Hilton Reservation Service.

Bay Point
Panama City
Florida

Bay Point is a new resort located four miles south-west of Panama City on St. Andrews Bay. It is a condominium-type

Clint Eastwood playing in the Invitational Celebrity Tournament at The Beach and Tennis Club in Pebble Beach, California.

development with tennis, golf, and a marina as its three main attractions. Besides these, several swimming pools, good beaches, an 18-hole miniature golf course, and a children's playground and day-care center make this a very agreeable holiday haven.

Accommodation is in one, two or three bedroom villas scattered throughout the property and overlooking either the water or the golf course. All villas have kitchens. There is a central clubhouse containing the main dining room, cocktail lounges, sauna and steam baths. The whole property is surrounded by two championship 18-hole golf courses.

Twelve soft granule courts are available to guests, at a cost of $2.00 per person per hour. There is also a well equipped pro-shop with restringing facilities and a good selection of the latest tennis fashions. The tennis pro, Gene Nolan gives private lessons at $7.00 per half-hour lesson. Visiting professionals often conduct clinics and exhibition matches. There are also special children's clinics during school vacation periods.

For further information contact Mr. Tom Molloy, Vice President, Operations. The telephone number is 904-234-3307.

The Belleview Biltmore

Belleair
Clearwater, Florida 33517

The Belleview Biltmore is a private resort estate and hotel in the residential community of Belleair, some two miles south of Clearwater. The hotel is a seasonal operation, open from early January until late April and is conducted on a full American Plan (all meals included). Rates here are higher than average, but the accommodations, food, service and facilities are also better than average.

There are six har-tru courts which are always kept in top-top condition. Two professionals, Michael Gaylorde, the head pro and Jean Bourdeau, the assistant professional, give private lessons, arrange compatible games and organize weekly mixed round robins. The courts are lighted for night play and have to be reserved a day in advance, but there is no charge for their use. A private lesson costs $12 per hour; group lessons are

The Del Monte Lodge in Pebble Beach, California has a long history of tennis enthusiasm — the first Davis Cup originated here. Although a private club the eleven plexipave courts are made available to guests at the Lodge.

arranged on request. Racquet restringing is done on the premises and there is a well stocked pro-shop.

In addition to tennis, the Biltmore offers two championship eighteen-hole golf courses, swimming in the temperature-controlled pool, as well as a Gulf of Mexico Cabana Club, deep-sea fishing, plus a complete social program within the hotel itself. On two recent occasions, the Annual Meeting of the USLTA has been held here. The hotel is well known in the tennis world.

For more information contact Mr. Donald E. Church, Manager. The telephone number is 813-442-6171.

Club Longboat — Beach and Tennis

5055 *Gulf of Mexico Drive*
Longboat Key
Sarasota, Florida 33577

Club Longboat is a tropical condominium project located on Longboat Key, across the bay from Sarasota. Longboat Key is a ten-mile-long island on the Gulf of Mexico. It has beautiful white sand beaches and its inhabitants claim that the average yearly temperature is seventy-three degrees.

At Club Longboat, the tennis enthusiast enjoys a total tennis environment. A clubhouse with a sauna, bar and pool is provided. Championship tennis courts (ten) are scattered throughout the property, which is palm-studded and very beautiful. The courts are surfaced with the new American bilt-right turf, which is similar to artificial grass. It has been specifically designed for tennis and has all the advantages of grass and clay — it is easy on the feet, yet fast.

The head professional is Joan Benton who gives private lessons at a cost of $7.50 for half an hour. Group lessons are given when there is a demand for them. There are occasional tournaments for guests, again when there is a demand for them. There are no regular tennis clinics. A well stocked pro-shop with restringing facilities is part of the tennis picture. To join the Tennis Club there is a charge of $25 per week per family for renters of condominiums only; no outside daily or weekly members are admitted.

Other club facilities include a beautiful six-hundred-foot Gulf of Mexico beach, a marina, a teenage center and two swimming pools.

The Sarasota area abounds with things to do — good restaurants, parks, fishing, water skiing, shopping centers (St. Aumand Circle, four miles from Club Longboat, has one hundred shops). Sarasota is also the art center of Florida.

For children, the Sarasota Jungle Gardens, the Circus Hall of Fame, The Glass Blowers, Floridaland and the Ringling Circus Winter Quarters are a constant source of amusement.

All the apartments are air conditioned, three-bedroom, two-bath, multi-terraced units and have been designed in a very attractive Mediterranean-style around a central courtyard.

For information regarding renting or buying contact Ms. C. W. Cunningham at Club Longboat.

Country Club Inn

Palm Tree Boulevard
Cape Coral
Florida 33904

The Country Club Inn is advertised as "A little out of the way, a little out of this world". It is located approximately fifty miles south of Sarasota on the Gulf of Mexico and is a medium-size hotel of approximately 150 rooms, surrounded by an eighteen-hole Dick Wilson golf course, palm-studded gardens, swimming pool and tennis courts.

A million-dollar Yacht and Racquet Club offers every amenity to the sailing and tennis enthusiast. There are five har-tru courts here, two of which are lighted for night play. A tennis professional, a complete pro-shop, changing and shower facilities, bar, restaurant and lounging area complete the tennis picture. There is no charge for use of the courts for hotel guests. They do have to be reserved, and playing time is limited to one hour per reservation.

Besides sailing, the Yacht Club also offers skin diving, deep-

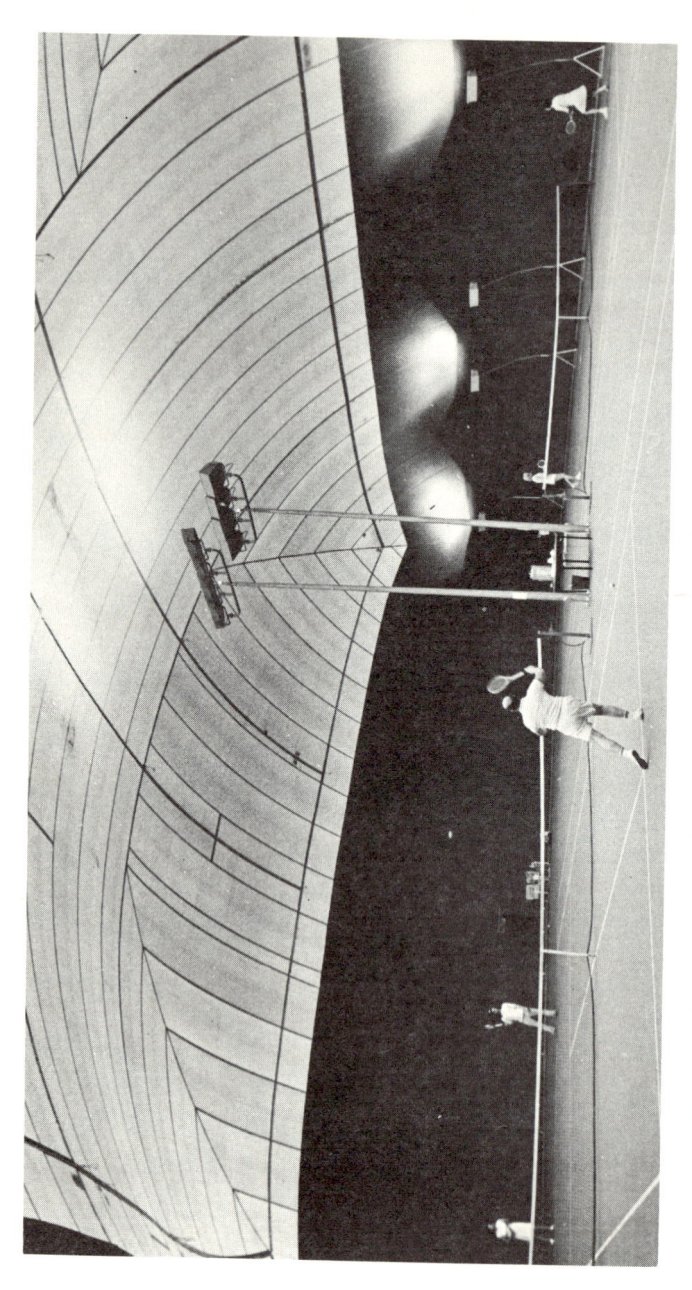

Two of the six all-weather tennis courts at The Broadmoor in Colorado Springs are covered by a bubble for winter play, thus making it possible to ski and to play tennis on the same day.

sea fishing, fresh-water fishing, and swimming. A wide, clean stretch of beach, bocci courts, putting green, one of the best marinas in Florida, and a good international cuisine all attract vacationers to the Inn and away from the hurly burly of Miami Beach. Here the pace is slower and the prices are lower than on Miami Beach.

For more information write to the Manager.

The Diplomat Hotel and Country Club
Hollywood-by-the-Sea
Florida

The Diplomat, a large Florida hotel, has a thousand-foot oceanfront beach, an Intercoastal Waterway with complete boating and fishing facilities, top-star entertainment (Dionne Warwick, Liza Minelli, Isaac Hayes, Peggy Lee, Englebert Humperdinck) in the elegant Café Cristal, and an excellent cuisine.

There are twelve all-weather tennis courts (two are lighted for night play) adjacent to the Country Club. It is necessary to reserve the courts, particularly in the high season when doubles are permitted for one hour at a time, and singles half an hour. There are no fees for hotel guests. Visitors are charged $3 per person per day.

A full-time teaching professional, Pepe Aguero, (Cuban champion for nine years and a Davis Cup player) and his two assistant professionals, Tom Bowden and Gerry Perlman, give lessons. The charge for individual lessons for adults, juniors or children is $12 for half an hour. There are no group lessons. There is an excellent pro-shop, offering in addition to tennis equipment and clothing, a racquet restringing and repair service.

Tournaments — boys and girls, men's doubles, ladies' doubles and mixed doubles are scheduled every Christmas.

There are also two eighteen-hole championship golf courses (and clubhouse with locker and shower facilities) — The Diplomat Country Club and The Presidential which are open to guests.

The Diplomat is located midway between Fort Lauderdale and Miami Beach in Hollywood-by-the-Sea.

For more information write to Ms. Audrey Bryan at The Diplomat Hotel.

Doral Country Club

Miami Beach
Florida

The Doral Country Club is a large luxury complex comprising an area of over 2400 acres. The basic concept of the overall design is a circle of buildings around a lake. This circle is made up of the Clubhouse and eight guest lodges. A very new resort, Doral offers to the sports-minded vacationer superb golf and tennis facilities in a lush country setting not far from the bright lights of Miami Beach.

There are nine clay and ten hard courts here. There is no charge to hotel guests for their use, but they do have to be reserved one day in advance. Playing time is limited to one hour per reservation. However, getting enough court time is seldom, if ever, a problem.

The resident professional is Uriel Oquando. A half-hour private lesson costs $15, a one-hour lesson $30. There are special tennis clinics every Monday, Wednesday and Friday which are a bargain at $5 per person per hour. Elwood Cooke, the visiting pro and Arthur Ashe, the touring pro, often assist at these clinics.

Guest tournaments are held every Thursday, with gala trophy presentations on Fridays. There is a very well equipped clubhouse next to the tennis courts with a pro-shop and racquet restringing facilities. Tennis is a well organized sport at Doral and the caliber of play is high.

The Doral Country Club is one of a new and ever-increasing type of Florida luxury hotel offering wonderful tennis in addition to the usual superb golf, and lively night life. Winter rates, double occupancy, MAP, range from $59 to $89 per day, summer rates are slightly cheaper at $54 to $84. For further information phone toll free 800-327-6334 (from any point in the United States), otherwise phone 305-592-2000, or write to the Reservations Manager.

You can mix business with pleasure at the Washington Hilton — an active in-town resort with three good har-tru tennis courts.

Lake Worth Racquet and Swim Club

4090 *Cocoanut Road*
Lake Worth
Florida 33460

Strictly a club with no accommodations, the Lake Worth Racquet and Swim Club makes short-term arrangements for non-residents and visitors. The weekly rate is $20 per person and the monthly rate is $70 per person. During Christmas and Easter weeks, tennis facilities for short-term and seasonal members are limited from 11 a.m. to 3 p.m. on week days, except when accompanied by a resident member. Summer short-term membership rates are considerably less.

The Club has ten courts; eight are clay and two are all-weather. All the latest teaching aids are here; ball machines, video-tape replays, etc. Private lessons are available. There are numerous round robins, inter-club and team matches, challenge ladders, and women's leagues. The caliber of tennis is very high here and there is great enthusiasm for the game.

A clubhouse with pro-shop, changing facilities and showers, bar and restaurant, and a huge olympic-size swimming pool are on the premises. For more information write to Mr. William Esser, Manager.

Marco Beach Hotel and Villas

Marco Island
Florida 33937

Marco Island is the largest of the 10,000 islands off the Gulf Coast of Florida. Although secluded and peaceful, it is connected to the mainland by two bridges so that one can drive from Miami in less than two hours. There are also five daily flights from Miami to the Marco Island Airport.

The Marco Beach Hotel is a large ten-storied hotel. Besides all the usual big hotel amenities and luxuries, its main appeal lies in the fact that it is the only hotel on a beautiful stretch of white-sand beach. The water is clean and clear and the beach is uncrowded.

Golf on two 18-hole championship golf courses, wonderful fishing for sailfish, dolphin, kingfish, tarpon and sea trout, sailing (instruction is available), a good children's program and a variety of dining rooms and cuisines to choose from — these are the main attractions of Marco Island. And, of course, tennis. There are a total of seventeen soft-composition courts, with some lights for night play. They are free to hotel guests, but there is a small charge for lights. The Tennis Pro Shop has a complete line of fashions, accessories, and racquets. Racquets can be restrung here. Courts are reserved a day in advance and getting enough court time is not a problem.

There are four pros — Ernie Stiller, President of the Florida Professional Tennis Association is the head professional. Others are Carol Stiller, Patty Szakal and Phyllis Roach. A private half-hour lesson costs $10.00.

The Hotel has a variety of accommodations, from housekeeping cottages to hotel rooms to penthouse suites. Winter rates for a double room, European Plan are $55 per day, for a two-bedroom villa on the golf course $120 per day. There are also cheaper seven-night rates. For more information write to Ms. Martha Raho at the Hotel, or phone 813-394-2511.

Meed Racquet Club

7625 Meed Drive
Lake Worth
Florida 33460

Scheduled for completion at the end of 1974, the Meed Racquet Club is going to be one of the largest tennis developments in the United States. Among the features to be included are thirty-four tennis courts (including four indoor and air conditioned), 1228 apartment and townhouse units, an exhibition stadium for 1500 spectators expandable for an additional 1500, and a plush, three-story clubhouse with all health-club facilities, pro-shop, specialty shops, dining rooms, bar, and billiard room.

The site comprises 121 acres but only twenty-one acres are to be covered by buildings. The rest will be parkland with man-

Michael Gaylorde, the professional, with William McChesney Martin (right) former Chairman of the Federal Reserve Board, at The Belleview Biltmore in Clearwater, Florida. Four har-tru courts with lights are maintained in tiptop condition for both day and night play.

made lakes, waterways, swimming pools, putting greens, and children's play areas.

All accommodation will be in housekeeping units, either for sale or rent. Full hotel accommodations are to be had at the Country Squire Inn, a new 114-unit motor inn located next door to the Racquet Club.

Fred Fleming has been named tennis director and head professional. He has already coordinated a complete tennis program for future residents and outside members. Among the activities planned are weekly tournaments and clinics for members, residents, and guests. The Club also hopes to host local and nationwide tournaments. At present, a vacation package is offered at $375 per person per week ($175 for a non-playing spouse) which includes breakfast and dinner and an intensive program of tennis instruction and supervision.

For more information telephone 305-968-4050 or write to the Reservations Manager.

Ponte Vedra Club

Ponte Vedra Beach
Florida 32082

Twenty miles south of Jacksonville, spectacularly set on its own mile-long beach, surrounded by a twenty-seven hole golf course, three swimming pools and ten tennis courts, stands the Ponte Vedra Club, a first-class luxury vacation resort. The Inn and its cottages and seaside buildings can accommodate approximately three hundred and the Club's grounds comprise one-thousand acres. The Ponte Vedra operates on a club membership plan. Reservations are accepted from club members, sponsored guests of members and from former guests. A non-resident membership costs $12 per year.

There are ten all-weather courts, open from 8 a.m. until dark, seven days a week, all the year around. The tennis pro is "Z" Mincek, a former Yugoslav Davis Cup player, who, with his assistant Mike Hutfield does an excellent job of giving lessons and organizing games. A half-hour private lesson costs $10. There are no group lessons, but clinics are held on a weekly basis as well as guest tournaments and round robins. Guests and members of the Club pay $2.00 per hour per person per court; non-members pay $3.00. A fully equipped pro-shop with restringing and rental facilities, lockers, showers, bar, snack service, air conditioned lounge, youth activity room, and spectator tiers for 150 people, complete the tennis picture. There are two tennis houseparties every year — in October and in January. This is the biggest tennis club for miles around and the courts are always busy. Three more courts are being built. Court time is by reservation only and is limited to one hour. The courts do not have lights.

Price of accommodations varies with the season, starting at $46 for a double room in the low season, and going up to $68 for an oceanfront room in the high season (December to April). This includes breakfast and dinner.

Stretching luxuriously along a vast expanse of oceanfront, here is Florida at its best, quiet and elegant.

For more information write to Ms. Elaine B. Koehl at the Ponte Vedra Club.

Sabin-Mulloy Tennis Camp

Lake Nellie Road
Clermont, Florida 32711

The Sabin-Mulloy Tennis Camp is owned by Wayne Sabin and Gardnar Mulloy, two famous names in tennis. It is a resident summer camp for boys and girls of ages nine to sixteen. Beginners, intermediate and advanced players are all welcome. In the winter months there are similar programs for adults.

Tucked away on lovely Lake Nellie, the large, lush acreage is completely secluded from the outside world. The main house and guest cottages are nestled in a luxuriant park-like setting and are located next to a lake which is filled with wide-mouthed bass, perch and other game fish.

The tennis curriculum claims to develop the aspirant faster than any other method. One of their methods is to take the top male and female players of the last fifty years and to examine their outstanding traits, to see if there are common denominators in the big four areas of their game: mechanics, tactics, psychology and physical set-up. When thus analyzed, certain essential truths of the game emerge and how it should be played and taught. These are the principles that are taught at the Sabin-Mulloy Camp.

Other activities include swimming, boating, fishing, water skiing, horseback riding and trips to Disney World and Cape Kennedy.

The fee per two-week session is $395 for the children's program and $295 for a weekly adult session. Make your reservations early; the Sabin Mulloy Camp fills up quickly. For more information write to Mr. Gardnar Mulloy at the Camp.

Sheraton Beach

19400 *Collins Avenue*
Miami Beach
Florida 33160

A sprawling complex of hotel, villas, swimming pools, children's playground, tennis courts, and a beautiful wide-sand beach, the Sheraton has a casual charm that is unique in Miami Beach. It is an ideal place to bring children or teenagers for a holiday because the social staff of the hotel runs extensive programs for them, leaving parents free to enjoy the six clay tennis courts.

Four of the courts are spectacularly set on the ocean's edge and the view and sea breezes make playing on them a delight. The head professional is Martin Buxby (formerly ranked number ten in the United States) and Frank Ackley is the assistant pro. A half-hour lesson costs $12; there are no regularly scheduled group lessons, but seasonal (Christmas, Easter, etc.) clinics are held for hotel guests. There is no charge for use of the courts, which are for hotel guests only. There is a well-stocked pro-shop. Reservations have to be made a day ahead and playing time is limited to one hour during the busy season (December to April). Rental racquets and equipment are available and restringing is done on the premises.

An old barn was transported lock, stock, and barrel from Ohio and has been converted into The Grist Mill, a really charming

Seventeen fast-dri composition courts, two lighted for after-dark play, attract tennis buffs to Marco Beach Hotel and Villas in Florida.

restaurant, with open-hearth cookery as its specialty. Nearby are all the attractions of Miami Beach; golf courses, jai alai, horse racing, and big-name entertainment. For information on rates write to Mr. Chuck Thiess, General Manager.

Silver Thatch Racquet Club
529 *North Ocean Boulevard*
Pompano Beach
Florida 33062

The Silver Thatch Racquet Club is a wonderful place for a Florida tennis holiday. Set in nine acres of tropically landscaped gardens, it extends from the Atlantic Ocean to the Intracoastal Waterway. It is thirty-five miles away from Palm Beach and Miami and only nine miles away from Fort Lauderdale. The Club itself is directly on the ocean with a lovely five-hundred-foot stretch of private beach. Apartments, villas and the Main Lodge overlook the Atlantic. There is a casual country club atmosphere here which makes it easy to meet people and to have a good time.

There are ten har-tru tennis courts here. The head professional, Ian Laver and the assistant pro, Gene Breasnell give private and group lessons and conduct special clinics on request. A private lesson from Ian Laver costs $12; from Gene Breasnell $10. There are, however, special lesson packages. A one-and-a-half hour group lesson (four people) costs $12 per person. Many round robins and professional tournaments are staged here — this is a very active tennis center. Racquet restringing is not done on the premises, but repair services are nearby and racquets are back in one day. There is no charge for use of the courts for hotel guests and Club members, but non-members pay $5 per day during the off season and $8 in the high season. The courts are not lighted. A complete pro-shop and clubhouse are part of the tennis facilities. The Silver Thatch Racquet Club is one of the best tennis resorts in the United States.

Two swimming pools, shuffleboard, a poolside patio, cocktail lounges and a good dining room are other features of the Club.

The choice of accommodations is wide; efficiencies, bedroom apartments, villas and hotel rooms. The hotel can accommodate 140 people. Prices vary with type of accommodation and the season. A double room in the Main Lodge, without meals, costs $26 in the high season, but only $10 from April 23 to December 12. To be able to take advantage of the low rates a ten-day minimum stay is required during the off season.

For more information write to Ms. Ann O'Brien at the Club.

Sonesta Beach Hotel

350 *Ocean Drive*
Key Biscayne
Florida 33149

Whether your mood is for a lazy day on the beach, basking in the sun with the roar of surf in your ears, a rousing tennis match, or a swinging bust-out night of music and dancing, you will find them all at the Sonesta Beach Hotel. Less than a twenty-minute drive from Miami International Airport, Key Biscayne is worlds away from the hustle and bustle of the Florida mainland.

The Sonesta is a typical large Florida hotel and it has all the amenities of a large hotel — swimming pool, good beach, sailing, snorkeling, fishing and golf. The Key Colony Golf Club is very near and the new Key Biscayne golf course is only a three-minute drive away. Golf lessons are available at both places.

The Sonesta Beach has eight all-weather tennis courts, a tennis club and a pro-shop. The National Teaching Pros hold their conventions here from time to time. A sanctioned pro tournament; the Sonesta-Saga Mini Grand Prix; the Key Biscayne branch of the Florida Ladies Tennis Tournament League; the second tournament in the annual Orange Bowl Festival consisting of amateur junior players from all over the world; and numerous local tournaments are all held here. The pro's name is Patricio Apey, a former Davis Cup player from Chile.

Besides tennis, the area offers practically every activity one can think of — from visiting the parrot jungle to organized beachcomber hikes. Horse racing, jai alai, the Miami Seaquarium (home of Flipper), and the many kennel clubs in the area are all well worth seeing.

The Sonesta Beach is a terrific place for children because many special outings and activities are arranged just for them. For information on prices, which vary greatly with the seasons, write to Ms. Joan Du Barry Fisher at the Sonesta Beach Hotel.

The Tennis Club of Palm Beach
2800 *Haverhill Road North*
West Palm Beach
Florida 33401

Scheduled for completion in the fall of 1974, The Tennis Club of Palm Beach will be a large condominium-town house project offering to its members and guests excellent tennis facilities. This is a private club and those wishing to join as non-resident members may do so by paying the initiation fee of $500. Annual dues are $350 a year. All memberships are family memberships. Besides tennis, facilities include squash courts, an olympic-size swimming pool, complete clubhouse with restaurant, lounge and bar, and men's and women's locker rooms each with showers and saunas.

There will be thirty-three har-tru "quick-dry" tennis courts, each individually fenced with adjoining covered cabanas with tables and chairs, water coolers and telephones. There will be no charge for use of the courts, four of which will be lighted for night play. A fully equipped pro-shop with a resident teaching professional are part of the tennis complex. The professional is Yvon Le Blanc. A half-hour private lesson costs $7.00. Regular tournaments and children's programs are in the planning stages.

The forty-acre site is only six miles away from the Worth Avenue shopping area, seven miles from the Atlantic Ocean, and three miles away from the Palm Beach Lakes Golf Center. Accommodation will be in one, two, or three-bedroom apartment units, or in two-bedroom townhouses scattered throughout the property. Prices of units are $33,900 for a one-bedroom apartment, $54,900 for a two-bedroom townhouse and $77,900 for a three-bedroom apartment. Monthly maintenance charges will range from $34 to $68. Eighty percent, twenty-five year financing is available. For more information write to Mr. Dennis Burchell or telephone 305-683-6371.

The Cloister

Sea Island, Georgia

The famous Cloister Hotel on Sea Island has long been a mecca for vacationers who desire a variety of diversions, fabulous food and a restful unhurried atmosphere. Spectacularly set among gardens and quiet terraces of trees and flowering semitropical shrubs, The Cloister, with its 205 rooms, is one of the great old-fashioned family hotels. Sea Island itself, is still quite unspoiled. Many private vacation homes along a five-mile stretch of beach can be rented through the Hotel.

There are fourteen Teniko (all-weather) courts here and three professionals. The head pro is Gus Peeples, who, together with his assistants, Mike Clapp and David McLean, runs the tennis show. Both private and group lessons are available. Private lessons cost $16 per hour; group lessons for six people cost $24 per hour. During the summer months there are weekly tennis clinics for juniors. For adults, there are weekly round robins in the spring and summer. There is a charge for use of the courts — $4 per hour per court for guests and cottagers, and $6 for outsiders. Courts have to be reserved a day in advance. A clubhouse has changing and shower facilities and the proshop does restringing. Tennis is played all the year around, as are all other outdoor sports.

Other sports include golf (thirty-six holes with a beautiful ante-bellum clubhouse), three skeet ranges and excellent horses and trails for riding. The hotel has a total of fifty mounts for hire. All the water sports are here as well; sailing, water skiing, fishing, snorkeling and skin diving.

The Cloister operates on full American Plan with rates for two persons ranging from $49 to $87 daily. For more information contact Mr. S. C. Kaufman, Manager.

The Racquet Club at Ponte Vedra, Florida is the heart of tennis activity for miles around. Mr. Z. Mincek, a former Yugoslav Davis Cup player, is the Club's head professional.

Mauna Kea Beach Hotel
P.O. Box 218
Kamuela, Hawaii 96743

Stretching luxuriously under the bright Hawaiian sun, the internationally acclaimed Mauna Kea Beach Hotel is a true luxury resort. It was built by Laurence Rockefeller in the sixties and has since become world famous as a vacation paradise. Mauna Kea (meaning White Mountain because of the snow on its summit) is an extinct volcano. In a real sense it is also the highest of all mountains in the world, for although many others are higher above sea level, Mauna Kea starts from a great plain 18,000 feet below sea level and is built up from that as a single mountain rising within a distance of five miles to a height of nearly 32,000 feet. At 13,000 feet there is a small lake which often freezes.

The Hotel has 256 air-conditioned rooms ranging in price from $90 to $100 daily with breakfast and dinner. There are, however, package plans which are considerably cheaper. The architecture of the main and outlying buildings is excitingly modern, with many outdoor living and eating spaces, and glass, shrubs and flowers used to great effect. The hotel offers a dizzling array of continental, American and Hawaiian food. Dress is extremely informal, except in the evening, when a jacket for the men and cocktail dresses for the women are *de rigueur*.

The area is noted for its dry, tropical climate, receiving an annual rainfall of less than seven inches. This makes it the driest inhabited area in Hawaii. It is 150 air miles south-east of Honolulu and is reached via Hawaiian Airlines from Honolulu.

Mauna Kea offers a variety of sports and outdoor activities, including golf on an eighteen-hole Robert Trent Jones championship course, horseback riding, hunting for pheasant, boar and bighorn sheep, surfing, snorkeling, sailing and deep-sea fishing. In nearby Waimea, the hotel maintains a riding stable where guided trail tours through the cool Kohala Mountains (3000-foot elevation) are arranged.

There are nine all-weather tennis courts. The professionals

are John Somerville and Henry Kamakana. The tennis fee is $2 per person per hour. Tennis is played all the year around. (The hottest months are August and September, the coolest months January and February with an average temperature of seventy-five degrees F.) Courts must be reserved a day ahead of time and playing time is limited to one hour. A substantial pro-shop, changing and shower facilities, bar and snack restaurant are part of the tennis complex.

Interesting landmarks in the area are Puukohola Heiau, one and a half miles away, petroglyph fields (ancient stone writings) three miles away, and the Hawaii Volcano National Park. For more information contact Mr. Nikolaus O. Klotz, Manager.

Sun Valley

Sun Valley
Idaho 83353

A large sporting complex well known throughout the world as a winter sports center, Sun Valley has in recent years developed into a summer sports haven as well. Situated in the beautiful mountain country of Idaho, Sun Valley offers to the summer vacationer a wide choice both in activities and accommodations. Accommodations are in either The Sun Valley Lodge, The Inn, apartments or condominiums.

There are eighteen tennis courts, including a teaching court with instant video-replay, a practice court with two pitching machines and the only grass court in the western United States. In the pro-shop, hostesses sell a full range of tennis supplies and fashions and restringing is done here. They also schedule games and arrange suitable partners.

The Sun Valley Tennis School runs three three-week sessions from June to August for boys and girls from ages eight to eighteen. They can either board in a dormitory or stay with family or friends.

Adult programs of concentrated private instruction for three, five, or seven days can be arranged. Congenial round-robin tournaments for residents and guests are held on July and August weekends. Topflight exhibitions are put on by instructors and visiting professionals throughout the summer. Tennis is big at Sun Valley and competition is keen.

Paul Wilkins, a name well known in tennis circles for his ability to train winners, is the tennis professional. He charges $12 for a half-hour lesson, while the assistant pro charges $9. There is no charge for use of the courts for condominium owners or resort guests. Weekly mixed-doubles tournaments are held each Saturday afternoon, June 30 to September 1.

Other activities include golf on an eighteen-hole, 6,300 yard par 70 course. The front nine is designed to build the ego of the novice and to get the better player off to a good start. The back nine is more challenging. There is also a week-long golf camp for children.

For water sports, there are three heated swimming pools and Sun Valley Lake. Sailing, scuba diving, skin diving, water skiing and the latest rage, kayaking, are all popular. Horseback riding is taken seriously, with instruction available both in the English and Western saddles, as well as in jumping. The many mountain trails make riding a very pleasurable activity. Mountain-climbing lessons, float trips and an arts and crafts center are all growing in popularity.

The price of accommodations at the Lodge varies from $22 to $50 for a double room. At the Inn, a double room costs between $20 and $39. Apartments start at $50 a day and the price of condominiums varies between $23 for a studio suite to $80 a day for a four-bedroom cottage. If you can afford it, for a complete family vacation with every outdoor activity at your fingertips, Sun Valley is hard to beat.

The Don Kerbis Tennis Ranch

R.R. No. 1 40-20
Watervliet
Michigan 49098

In an isolated spot near Watervliet, Michigan, one-hundred miles from Chicago, there is an expensive summer retreat where many world-class tennis players can be found every July and August. They are here to instruct approximately one-hundred children (and adults after the middle of August) who spend at least four hours a day in front of videotape cameras enthusiastically playing tennis. The staff consists of thirty-five persons, twenty-five of whom are tennis players. The rest are special counsellors chosen for their ability to get along with children, and to help with the swimming, horseback riding, canoeing, arts and crafts, and drama programs. The camp strives for a well balanced program of activities with special emphasis on tennis. Every day starts off with calisthenics or a mile jog, and a high protein breakfast.

Students and staff live in cabins equipped with electricity, bunk beds, screened windows, showers and toilets. Rates are $500 for a three-week session and $200 for adults for a one-week session. Boys and girls from ten to eighteen, from beginning tennis players to advanced, participate in this program to the great improvement of their game. This camp is the only tennis camp fully accredited by the American Camping Association.

For more information write to:

Winter Address: Don Kerbis Tennis Club, 1660 Skokie Valley Road, Highland Park, Illinois.

Summer address: The Don Kerbis Tennis Ranch, R.R. No. 1 40-20, Watervliet, Michigan 49098, Telephone (616) 463-3151

Grand Hotel

Mackinac Island
Michigan

The Grand Hotel claims to be the world's largest summer hotel, and after one has seen the enormous building and the white-columned, eight-hundred-foot porch, one can well believe this claim. The grounds cover five-hundred acres and adjoin the sixteen-hundred acres of the Mackinac Island State Park. There are 350 guest rooms. The Hotel is open from May until October and has a long history as a popular family vacation spot. Reservations must be made well in advance.

There is a nine-hole golf course on the hotel grounds, together with a putting green, clubhouse and pro-shop. Caddies are

Anna-Marie Pinto Bravo of Chile playing in the Sonesta-Saga Bay Mini Grand Prix at the Sonesta Beach Hotel on Key Biscayne, Florida.

available. Other activities include: swimming in the heated swimming pool (Esther Williams was photographed in a series of water-ballet sequences in this pool), riding on lovely secluded bridle paths, bingo, bridge parties, baseball, bicycling and nightly dancing in the Terrace Room.

Four har-tru tennis courts are available to guests. There is no charge for use of the courts, which are not lighted. The professional, Frank Foster, charges $7 for a half-hour lesson. There is a pro-shop which has equipment for sale or rent. Round robins are arranged when there is a demand for them, but the big yearly tournament is held in August — The Mackinac Island Tennis Tournament. Guests of the hotel and ranking amateur players from various parts of Canada and the United States enter.

There are no cars on Mackinac Island, which makes it ideal for either bicycling or horse-drawn carriage rides. (Automobiles are forbidden by law.) Time should also be spent visiting the island's historical sites and in leisurely shopping expeditions in the village, which is full of antique and handicraft shops.

The Grand Hotel is in the medium price range, operating on full American Plan. For more information write to Mr. G. Gibbs, Reservations Manager, 222 Wisconsin Avenue, Lake Forest, Illinois 60045.

Irish Hills Tennis Camp

P.O. Box 6886
Grosse Pointe, Michigan 48236

The Irish Hills Tennis Camp is conducted on the campus of Hillsdale College in the Irish Hills of South Michigan. Accommodation is in one of the student residences in comfortable, air conditioned rooms. These are designed to accommodate either married couples or single men and women. Most of the rooms have their own bathroom. This program is held every summer in weekly sessions from the middle of June until the middle of August. There are also two special four-day tennis weekends.

The program includes six hours of daily supervised practice. There is both group and individual instruction with tournaments, strategy sessions and class lessons. Joseph Felice is the Camp Director and head professional. Six outdoor all-weather courts and three indoor courts are used for practice sessions. The student-instructor ratio is kept at four to one, which makes the teaching program very effective. This is an adult tennis camp and children are not admitted.

Rates are $250 per person per week, or $175 per person for a four-day weekend. The fees include all meals, lodging, instruction, and other camp activities. For more information contact Ms. Anne W. Rosch, Business Manager or phone 313-821-1922. The summer telephone number is 517-437-3311.

The Frontier

Las Vegas
Nevada 89109

Well known for its famous casino, its exceptionally fine food, and its Howard Hughes connections, most people do not realize that The Frontier also offers excellent tennis facilities.

When you get tired of roulette and one-armed bandits, there are six laykold courts waiting outside. The courts are open and reservations are accepted from 7 a.m. to 10 p.m. all the year around. There is no charge for use of the courts for hotel guests. The pro is Gar Glenney who has been active in tennis promotion and tournaments for thirty years. The fee for a half hour of instruction is $8. A complete pro-shop featuring the latest in equipment and tennis fashions is on the premises. A clubhouse, showers and snack bar are part of the tennis complex.

After tennis you can cool off in the enormous three-sectioned pool; one section for waders, another for divers and the third for floaters. The Frontier also has guest privileges at one of the finest golf courses in Las Vegas. For information on rates, special packages and convention facilities write to the Director of Sales at The Frontier.

Mount Washington Hotel

Bretton Woods
New Hampshire 03575

The *New Yorker* called it "one of the great bargains of our time". It was referring to the Rod Laver-Roy Emerson tennis clinics at the Mount Washington Hotel in scenic Bretton Woods in New Hampshire.

This hotel was built in 1902, and although modernized since then, a huge verandah and other traces of that more leisurely era still exist. The Presidential Range can be seen in the distance. In front of the hotel is a small stream, the Ammonoosuc and ten tennis courts.

There are many other things to do — there is a championship eighteen-hole golf course, indoor and outdoor swimming pools, a sauna, riding and trout fishing.

A total of eight weekly tennis clinics are held here, starting the second week in July. All-day instruction, automatic ball machines, video-tape closed-circuit television, and most importantly, Rod Laver, Roy Emerson and Fred Stolle are features of these clinics.

The clinics are a big attraction for tennis players. Surprisingly, the big pros actually do spend all day coaching and playing, and with eight courts constantly in use, the thirty or forty people taking part get their fill of tennis. At approximately $325 per week, including all meals, this is truly a bargain. It is open to everybody seventeen years of age and over. A special rate for a non-tennis playing spouse is available.

Information on other details may be obtained by writing to The Rod Laver Tennis Clinic at the Hotel.

The Monmouth

Spring Lake Beach
New Jersey 07762

The Monmouth is a large seaside resort hotel situated on the busy New Jersey shore. It offers an extensive social program — get acquainted cocktail parties, nightly dances, movies, card parties, Sunday-night concerts, fashion shows and other similar activities typical of large hotels.

There are three clay tennis courts here. A professional is on duty to give lessons and to arrange foursomes. There is a charge of $2 an hour per court for hotel guests and $3 an hour per court for outsiders. A small pro-shop with rental equipment is on the premises. Courts have to be reserved and playing time is limited to one hour.

An eighteen-hole putting green is on the hotel grounds and two excellent golf courses are within a mile of the hotel. The Monmouth Park Racetrack is nearby, as is some very good deep-sea fishing. The beach is white and clean. There is also a large swimming pool.

Daily rates for two people, including breakfast and dinner range from $56 to $72. The hotel is open from June 20 to Labor Day.

Concord Hotel

Kiamesha Lake
New York 12751

The Concord is a large summer hotel with all the usual amenities of a Catskill resort — a lovely lake for water sports, heated swimming pool, three golf courses, nightly entertainment of just about every kind, and a very active children's program.

Tennis, however has become *the* sport at the Concord and the hotel takes pride in its terrific tennis facilities. There are thirteen outdoor courts (ten clay and three all-weather), meticulously maintained and supervised. There is no charge for use of the courts. There are also four indoor courts, a lounging area, locker rooms and showers in the Indoor Tennis House. This is unique in that it never closes. You may play at three o'clock in the morning if you wish. All courts, indoor and outdoor, have to be reserved.

Every Saturday afternoon a doubles exhibition game is staged, featuring well-known professionals. After the match, the pros conduct a clinic for hotel guests. The head pro here is Gary

Wilensky, who charges $12 for a half-hour lesson. The assistant pros charge $10 and group lessons cost $4 per hour. The staff has all the most modern equipment — special training racquets, ball-throwing machines, hand strengtheners, serving and groundstroke aids, stroke developers, rebound nets, instructional films, hand-wrist positioners, wrist developers, and a complete tennis library.

If it has anything at all to do with tennis, the pro-shop will have it, and at reasonable prices. If you are alone, the pro-shop is a good place to meet a partner. Usually it is very easy to find congenial games. Another feature of the pro-shop is the tennis films which are shown continuously and cover every aspect of the game from strokes to tactics. At the Concord tennis is taken seriously and a week here will do wonders for your game.

Rates are all full American Plan and there are many special packages. For more information write to the Manager.

High Hampton Inn and Country Club

Cashiers
North Carolina 28717

The High Hampton Inn and Country Club is a pleasant sprawling resort. It is an old-fashioned inn with cottages, set amid the wilds of the North Carolina mountains.

There are seven all-weather, fast-drying courts. Four of the courts have lights. There is no charge for use of the courts for hotel guests, but they have to be reserved a day in advance. A complete pro-shop, clubroom, showers and changing facilities are all here. A resident professional gives private lessons, holds clinics and arranges friendly round robins.

Besides tennis, the hotel has an excellent eighteen-hole, par 71 golf course with bent-grass greens. The High Hampton Inn is also famous for its excellent riding school and its many miles of riding trails. Other activities include boating, fishing and swimming.

Rates range from $20 to $23 per day, full American plan. Open from May until October, the High Hampton Inn and

Country Club is an ideal place for a family vacation, particularly for a family that is keen on tennis, golf, or riding. For more information, write to Mr. William D. McKee.

Tamiment Resort and Country Club
Tamiment
Pennnsylvania 18371

Tamiment, a large resort-convention hotel is located in the Pocono Mountains of Pennsylvania, eighty-five miles from New York City, ninety-five miles from Philadelphia and 230 miles from Washington, D.C. Very popular as a convention center, it is nevertheless a good family vacation spot, as it offers so many sports and entertainment facilities. Because the hotel is situated on the edge of a clean ninety-acre lake, all the water sports are available. There is an eighteen-hole championship golf course as well as handball, volleyball, shuffleboard, basketball, billiards and horseback riding. *Golf Digest Magazine* called the Robert Trent Jones designed golf course "one of America's most challenging courses".

Even the tennis facilities are on a grand scale. There are ten all-weather courts, all lighted for night play, as well as a complete pro-shop with all the latest teaching aids (ball machines, video-tape replays, etc.). The head professional here is Fred Ruzicka. He and his staff give lessons at $6 for a half-hour lesson. There is no charge for use of the courts for guests of the hotel. However, courts have to be reserved and playing time is limted to forty-five minutes at peak seasons. The courts are playable from May to October. Many tournaments are held throughout the season which guests are encouraged to enter. Restringing is done on the premises.

Tamiment has a total of 550 rooms, several cocktail lounges, a gift shop, a beauty salon, post office, health club and a fully staffed infirmary. Rates average around $70 double, full American Plan per day.

When one gets tired of all the sporting activities at Tamiment, the countryside is well worth exploring, with its interesting historical sites, summer theaters and scenic attractions.

John Newcombe and Ken Rosewall playing in the CBS Tennis Classic at Sea Pines Plantation on Hilton Head Island, South Carolina where tennis is played all the year around.

Sea Pines Plantation

Hilton Head Island
South Carolina

Sea Pines is unique. "A playground for people who take pride in the art of living — whether it's fishing, surfing, tennis, golf or bird watching. It's all better on the island and a notch slower than on the mainland." This was *Golf Magazine's* comment about Sea Pines. It is a 5200-acre luxury resort development situated on the southern tip of Hilton Head Island and its uniqueness lies in the excellence of its many sports facilities, the natural beauty of its surroundings, and its good overall design.

Sea Pines features fifty-four holes of the country's finest golf on its Ocean and Sea Marsh Courses, and on the famous Harbor Town Links designed by Pete Dye and Jack Nicklaus. Every year this course hosts the PGA Heritage Golf Classic.

There is horseback riding, sailing, fishing, water skiing, trap shooting, sailing and sunbathing along four miles of sunswept beaches. And, of course, tennis.

At Sea Pines tennis is played all year. It has, in fact, become famous for its big-name teaching pros and its excellent facilities. Both the men's and women's professional tours hold major tournaments here. Both the CBS Tennis Classic and the NBC Family Circle Cup are held at the Sea Pines Racquet Club. There are eighteen rubico (synthetic clay) and five all-weather courts. There is a charge of $2.00 per person per hour for use of the courts. Naturally there is a complete racquet club and pro shop, with lessons by appointment. Special clinics feature such names as Stan Smith, the Director of Tennis, Marty Riessen, Charles Pasarell, and others of the same caliber. Billie Jean King also plays here. There is a charge of $2 per person per hour for use of the courts.

The Sea Pines offers a wide range of accommodations. The Hilton Head Inn has two-hundred rooms, and in addition, there are hundreds of privately owned homes and villas which can be rented through the hotel.

Life at Sea Pines is easy and pleasant. *Fortune* described it very well — "A rare holdout against tasteless commercialism is Sea Pines Plantation".

For rates write to the Reservations Manager.

T-Bar-M Tennis Ranch
P.O. Box 469
New Braunfels
Texas 78130

The T-Bar-M Ranch is the home of 1973 U.S. Open Champion John Newcombe who often can be seen in action on one of the twenty-four laykold all-weather courts (four under cover and lighted). The T-Bar-M Ranch is unique because of its outdoor, away-from-the-crowd atmosphere, although it is only a few minutes' drive from the old German town of New Braunfels and an hour's drive from San Antonio with its many lovely old missions, the Alamo and lively Mexican night life.

There are two tennis programs here — the Mini and the Maxi Clinics. The Mini Clinic features tennis instruction in the mornings only, leaving the afternoons free to enter tournaments, swim, or just to relax. The Maxi Clinic is more intensive with its program of all-day instruction. The cost of the Mini Clinic is $12 per person per day, that of the Maxi Clinic $25 per day. Private lessons are available at a cost of $8 for a half-hour lesson. All the newest teaching aids are here — video recorders, ball machines, practice areas, and a daily "Tips on Tennis" session which is offered at no charge.

Both food and accommodation are simple, but good. Accommodation is in Western Cottages (suitable for families), Newcombe Lodge (hotel rooms), ranchettes (motel-type units), and in tennis villas which are the most luxurious. These have been built on a high ridge overlooking the ranch with fabulous views of the whole countryside. They are within easy bicycling or walking distance of the ranch. Rates are all European Plan, but include use of the tennis courts. A double room costs $25. A second room for the same family costs only $15. There is no charge for children under five. Three buffet-style meals cost $12 per person per day. The Ranch is open all year. For more information contact the Manager, or telephone 512-625-9105.

The Greenbrier

The Greenbrier
White Sulphur Springs
West Virginia 24986

Without a doubt, the Greenbrier is one of the great resorts of the world. It was first opened in 1778 and ever since has played host to the foremost figures of the political, social and sporting worlds of America. The place is steeped in history — Daniel Webster, Henry Clay, Robert E. Lee, Jefferson Davis and many other presidents of the United States have holidayed or have taken the cure here. Set in 6500 acres of rolling, wooded countryside, The Greenbrier emanates an aura of hospitality and comfort which is unusual in our day and age.

The Creative Arts Colony is located in a group of picturesque cottages that were built in 1813 by James Caldwell, then owner of White Sulphur Springs estate. Although the cottages have been restored, their design and architecture remain the same as when they were built a century and a half ago, with white-washed brick, handpegged floors and spacious piazzas. The Creative Arts Colony is open every weekday. The artists themselves demonstrate their special art or craft, whether it be painting, crewel designing, sculpting, potting, batik dyeing or weaving. Many articles are for sale and one can have items made to order.

The Greenbrier has good sports facilities — three eighteen-hole golf courses each beginning and ending at the clubhouse, olympic-size indoor and outdoor swimming pools, bowling lanes, combination trap and skeet fields, two-hundred miles of riding trails through pine-scented woods, and of course, tennis.

There are seventeen courts, fifteen with a har-tru and two with a hard all-weather surface. Two tennis professionals, Ray White and Peter Hemingway, give private lessons only. One half-hour lesson costs $7.00. Hotel tournaments are held regularly during the summer season, (mostly convention tournaments), but tennis can be played all year. A friendly clubhouse which serves snacks and drinks and a pro-shop with racquet restringing facilities and a full line of tennis equipment and

Fifteen har-tru and two all-weather courts provide ample tennis activity at West Virginia's famed Greenbrier which is set in 6500 acres of rolling, wooded countryside.

clothing are additional amenities. There is a charge of $2.50 per person per hour for use of the courts.

The Greenbrier has 650 rooms and prices vary according to season, type of accommodation, and plan. A large health spa is also on the premises. A double bedroom from November 20 to March 30, full American Plan costs $70. The same room from March 31 to November 15 costs $85 to $95. For more specific information write to Ms. Samantha Brown at The Greenbrier.

Club Méditerranée

The Club Méditerranée was founded as a sports association in 1950 by Gerard Blitz, a former member of the Belgian Olympic team, together with a group of his friends. The basic concept of the Club was, and still is, that city dwellers want to spend their vacations in a society and environment radically different from that of their daily lives. Attractive surroundings, abundant facilities for sports and recreation, live entertainment, French cuisine and a very informal life style are what the Club tries to provide its members.

The Club offers all-inclusive vacation packages. These include:
1. Roundtrip transportation (optional)
2. Accommodations
3. All meals, including wine with lunch and dinner
4. Free use of the Club's sports facilities, including such usually expensive sports as sailing, water skiing, scuba diving and deep-sea fishing and, in the winter, snow skiing
5. Free sports instruction by a permanent professional staff
6. Live entertainment; dances, cabarets
7. Transfers on specified group flights

There is no tipping and the only extras are drinks at the bar, personal purchases and special outings. Drinks are paid for with a string of multicolored poppet beads that can be worn around the neck. There is no need to carry money in the Club's cashless society and because all the basic elements of the vacation, as well as most of the activities are included in the price, members are freed from fears of running out of cash.

Accommodations are in resorts ranging from good to semi

luxurious. The following is a list of tennis centers operated by The Club Méditerranée. These are all bilingual. (English and French)
  Buccaneer's Creek in Martinique — 4 courts, 2 floodlit
  Fort Royal in Guadeloupe — 4 courts, 2 floodlit
  Moorea in Tahiti — 4 courts
  Agadir — 3 courts, Marrakesh — 3 courts, Yasmina — 4 courts, all floodlit, in Morocco
  Assinie on Africa's Ivory Coast — 4 courts, all floodlit
  D'jerba la Douce in Tunisia — 5 courts, 2 floodlit
  Pompadour in central France — 3 courts
  Cargese in Corsica — 7 courts
  Porto Petro in Majorca — 6 courts

All of these places offer an organized tennis program with group instruction by qualified professionals.

Today there are approximately 60,000 American and Canadian members of which 30,000 vacation with the Club every year. Memberships can be acquired through a travel agent and are valid for one year. A single membership costs $10, a family membership $14. For more information write to Ms. Sharon Wirz, Club Méditerranée Inc., 516 Fifth Avenue, New York, N.Y. 10036.

Playboy Clubs

Members of the Playboy Club are familiar with the attractions of Playboy resorts, but they may not be aware that three of them have excellent tennis facilities.

Playboy Club-Hotel at Great Gorge, McAfee, New Jersey

There are three indoor sportface, carpet-surface courts in the hotel's convention center. They are open from 9 a.m. until midnight. There is a charge of $8 an hour per court to hotel guests and $10 an hour for visitors.

Outdoors are four green urethane-covered asphalt courts with a spectator area. There is no charge for hotel guests, but visitors have to pay $4 an hour per court. A tennis professional is on duty the whole year around. Private and group lessons are available and there is a complete pro-shop on the premises, with restringing facilities.

Playboy Club-Hotel at Ocho Rios, Jamaica

Two asphalt courts are open from 8 a.m. until midnight, seven days a week, twelve months a year. There is no charge for hotel guests. The courts are lighted and a tennis professional conducts private and group lessons. Rental equipment is available.

Playboy Club-Hotel at Lake Geneva, Wisconsin

Four laykold courts with a spectator area are open from 9 a.m. to 7 p.m. seven days a week from May until October. The courts are not lighted. There is no charge for their use for hotel guests, but visitors have to pay $1.50 an hour per person.

Indoors, there are two carpet-surface courts in the hotel's convention area. A tennis professional is available only during the summer season. A pro-shop is on the premises.

For more information write to the Reservations Manager, Playboy Enterprises, Inc., The Playboy Building, 919 North Michigan, Chicago 60611.

TennisAmerica

TennisAmerica was founded in 1971 by Billie Jean King and her former instructor, Dennis Van der Meer. The concept has enjoyed almost instant success with branches all over the country offering the same special (and they claim, unique) teaching formula. TennisAmerica operates summer camps for juniors and adults, as well as tennis weeks and weekends in such diverse spots as The Golden Gate Tennis Club and The Leelanau Homestead in Michigan.

Although climate, quality of accommodations and sports amenities may vary from place to place, they all have one thing in common — tennis intensity. All programs offer at least four hours of free instruction or playing time per day, and there is no doubt that the TennisAmerica teaching system has produced many successful graduates.

Favorite winter spots are:

Golden Gate Tennis Club on San Francisco Bay California — very close to San Francisco and its many attractions. Excellent accommodations.

Port Royal Inn, Hilton Head Island, South Carolina — a quiet lush island which is rapidly becoming a great tennis center. Good restaurants, sailing, golf.

Safety Harbor Spa and Tennis Club, Safety Harbor, Florida — a health spa on the warm Gulf of Mexico bay featuring, besides tennis, mineral waters, free massages, whirlpool baths and a variety of entertainments including Disney World and jai alai nearby.

St. Lucie Hilton, Port St. Lucie, Florida — excellent golf, fishing and water sports. It is near West Palm Beach.

San Luis Bay Club, San Luis, Obispo, California — a beautiful oceanfront resort with championship golf, water sports and ten new tennis courts built exclusively for TennisAmerica.

Rates range from $148 for a weekend to $495 for a week, full American Plan, including all tennis instruction. Besides the above-mentioned places, TennisAmerica has many, many more. For a complete TennisAmerica information package phone (toll free) 800-228-9494 or write to TennisAmerica Inc., 1000 Elwell Ct., Palo Alto, California 94303.

CHAPTER 8
OTHER COUNTRIES

Sandpits Lawn Tennis Club
Sandpits
Gibraltar

Four years ago a landslide buried the entire tennis facility of the Sandpits Tennis Club. Happily, it has been rebuilt and boasts three new tennis-quick courts. The climate in Gibraltar is such that tennis can be played all year.

The Club has 430 members. There is a tremendous keenness for tennis, especially among the younger members. Visitors are welcome to use all Club facilities (bar, showers, pro-shop) by paying a small entrance fee of 25 p., approximately $1.00, and by signing themselves in. Guests share equal rights with members.

Gibraltar is full of excellent guest houses and small hotels. So, if you ever find yourself in Gibraltar and are looking for a tennis game, head for the Sandpits Lawn Tennis Club where you are assured of finding some very good and very friendly tennis players.

Bali International Golf and Tennis Center
Sanur
Bali, Indonesia

There is an excellent tennis club in Sanur, the main town in Bali, five-hundred miles away from Jakarta the capital of Indonesia. This is the Bali International Golf and Tennis Center. It consists of four new gravel courts, an eighteen-hole golf course and a clubhouse with its own Chinese restaurant. A pro-shop is in the clubhouse and a professional, Mr. Ir. Hadi gives lessons. All the courts are lighted for night play.

The Club is run for the convenience of guests at the Hotel Bali Beach (three-hundred rooms) and Bali Sea Side Cottages (sixty rooms). The courts are never crowded and playing time is unlimited. However, it is wise to reserve the preceding day. The climate is tropical. Do not come during the summer monsoon months. In the dry season, temperatures are cooler than most other tropical areas because the winter winds from Australia cool the island. Players are an interesting mixture of nationalities — Dutch, Eurasian, Chinese and the odd American tourist.

For more information write to the Manager.

Royal Tehran Hilton

P.O. Box 1526
Pahlavi Avenue/Parkway
Mahmoudieh
Tehran, Iran

The Royal Tehran Hilton is in the fashionable Shemiran residential district of Tehran, approximately five miles from the downtown area. The hotel runs a free bus service to the city for shopping and sightseeing. (Carpets, silks and fresh caviar are the outstanding buys here.) The Hotel has 550 modern air conditioned rooms, five restaurants serving international food, two bars and a heated swimming pool. There is one restaurant which specializes solely in Persian food. The hotel is set in an attractive landscaped garden with views of the city and the Alborz mountains.

Summers are hot and very dry. Temperatures can climb above the hundred mark. But in December, January and February, frosts are not uncommon. However, the extreme dryness of the air makes both these extremes bearable and tennis is played the whole year around.

There are four all-weather courts on the hotel grounds. There is no professional, but the demand for instruction is on the rise, and the hotel is planning to hire one in the near future. Racquets can be rented at $1.00 per hour. There is no charge for use of the courts.

Approximately a five-minute drive from the hotel is The Imperial Country Club which has a very active tennis section and which welcomes guests of the Hilton. There are professionals here and organized tournaments are held throughout the year. The Imperial Country Club also has an eighteen-hole golf course. Green fees are $5 on weekdays and $8 on holidays. There is a driving range and putting green and golf instruction is available.

Persian is the official language of Iran, but English, French and German are widely spoken. Dress during the day is casual, but a jacket and tie must be worn in the evening.

While in Iran, be sure to see the Golestan Palace, home of the Quajar kings. It is full of priceless Persian antiques and art treasures. Also well worth seeing are the crown jewels, the Bazaar, the Sepahsalar Mosque and a rug-washing ceremony. Excursions to the Caspian Coast, Isfahan, and Persepolis are easy to arrange. Isfahan has some of the world's loveliest Oriental architecture. Room rates are as follows: single $22 to $27, double $25.50 to $31, plus 15% service charge. These are European plan rates (meals are not included).

The Strand Hotel
Rosslare
County Wexford
Ireland

Advertised as the "sunniest and driest corner of Ireland", Rosslare is in the southeast section of Ireland. The surrounding area is full of little places of interest — sandy coves, quiet villages, antique shops, congenial pubs. For bird life Rosslare has few equals. The Saltee Islands Bird Sanctuary, Tern Island and Stoblands are fascinating to ornithologists and amateurs alike.

The village of Rosslare is small and quiet. The Rosslare eighteen-hole golf course, scene of many Irish Open Championships, stretches past six miles of sandy beach to Rosslare point and offers some exceptional scenery to the golfer.

The Strand Hotel has been managed by the Kelly family for three generations and although it is a large hotel by Irish standards (150 rooms) it has the friendliness and intimacy more often associated with small hotels. Food and wine are taken seriously here. Menus are varied and the portions are extremely generous. Fresh local fish and shellfish are house specialties. Wines, imported by the cask, are carefully chosen and are excellent value.

The hotel has a heated swimming pool, sauna, squash courts, massage and beauty parlors. Dinghy sailing is another popular activity.

There are two well maintained clay tennis courts, free to hotel guests. For more competitive tennis, there are nine clay courts in the village as well as a clubhouse, showers and pro-shop. Instruction is available both in the village and at the hotel. Tennis can be played all year. It is a very popular sport in this corner of the world and there are some excellent players here.

One of the Strand's most famous guests, George Bernard Shaw, had this to say about a holiday he spent here: "I was lost in dreams. One cannot work in a place where there is such infinite peace."

Rates, by American standards, are very reasonable but vary with the season. For more information write to Mr. William J. Kelly.

Dan Caesarea Golf Hotel

Caesarea
Israel

The Dan Caesarea, which claims to be Israel's most beautiful resort hotel, is located near the ancient port of Caesarea, about sixty-five miles from Tel Aviv on the Mediterranean coast. A large, very modern hotel, it has the great advantage of being so close to the magnificent Caesarea Roman ruins. The Roman aqueduct and amphitheatre are particularly outstanding. Two thousand years ago Caesarea was a large holiday resort. It was built to honor Caesar Augustus and its palaces and hippodromes resounded with life. Today, the remnants of this other life are being unearthed and pieced together by archeologists. Recently the ruins of an ancient race course were excavated. Exploring the ruins is a popular occupation of hotel guests.

Within the hotel grounds, and surrounded by a very pleasant garden, are two tennis courts. They are hard, all-weather courts, lighted for night play. There is a pro and a small pro-shop. There is no charge for use of the courts and playing time is unlimited. Courts do not have to be reserved.

Next door to the hotel is the eighteen-hole golf course. It is new, well maintained and challenging, set amid palm trees and gentle downs. There is a modern clubhouse. For information on rates write to the Manager.

Sri Lanka

Sri Lanka Tennis Association
45, Sir Marcus Fernando
Mawatha
Colombo 7
Sri Lanka

The Sri Lanka (formerly Ceylon) Lawn Tennis Association has eleven tennis courts at its headquarters at Edinburgh Crescent in Colombo. Two cement and two grass courts are located about a mile away. These courts are available to visitors upon payment of a small fee.

Tennis is very popular at several holiday resorts away from Colombo where temperatures range from cool to cold, such as The Kandy Garden Club on the Lake Road in Kandy, the Bandarawella Tennis Club in Bandarawella, the Nuwara Eliya Tennis Club in Nuwara Eliya and the Uva Club in Badulla.

Tennis is also available at two first-class hotels — Brown's Beach Hotel in Negombo on the coast, and Hunas Falls Hotel in Kandy, in the mountains where the climate is always temperate.

All visitors to Sri Lanka require a passport, inoculation certificates against cholera and yellow fever (if coming from infected areas), a return ticket and sufficient funds in foreign exchange for their maintenance while in Ceylon.

Legend has linked Sri Lanka with the Garden of Eden and it is a really exceptionally beautiful country with a vast variety of climates, cultures, vegetation, temples, ruins, natural beauties

The Nipa Lodge on Pattaya Beach in Thailand, south-east Asia's most popular beach resort, has two hard-surface courts which are floodlit for night play.

and animal life. For more tennis information write to the Sri Lanka Tennis Association.

The Nipa Lodge

Pattaya Beach
Cholburi
Thailand

The Nipa Lodge is named after a large Nipa palm in front of the hotel. Built on top of a hill and surrounded by tropical gardens stretching down to the sea, The Nipa Lodge is a luxurious retreat in the village of Pattaya, South East Asia's most popular beach resort on the east coast of the Gulf of Siam. It is approximately seventy miles from the nearest airport at Bangkok. The hotel's 150 rooms are all air conditioned and have their own bathrooms. There are a variety of dining rooms and bars including an English pub and the first discothèque in Thailand. The food is international with a Swiss chef presiding. Thai dancing and Thai food are features at a weekly barbecue.

There are two hard-surface courts, floodlit for night play. Lights are almost a necessity here because the heat of the day is so oppressive. There is no professional. A very pleasant bar has been set up next to the courts where players can sip long, cooling drinks. There is no charge for use of the courts and playing time is unlimited.

Trips to an underwater coral island, to the jungle to see elephants working in logging camps and to the Chantabury sapphire mines are interesting outings.

Guests at the Nipa Lodge are entitled to play golf at the Siam Country Club, the most beautiful course in the country. It is just a five-minute drive away.

All water sports — water skiing, diving, sailing, parasailing, fishing or cruising are available from the hotel beach. There is also an enormous swimming pool on the hotel grounds.

Monkeys and the odd elephant are part of the passing scene. They contrast strangely with the American modernity of the hotel. For more information write to Mr. K. Rufli, General Manager.

The Ankara Tennis Club
19 *Mayis Stadyomu*
Ankara
Turkey

The Ankara Tennis Club is the oldest tennis club in Turkey. Most Turkish champions come from this Club, and fortunately it is open to visitors. The charge for playing is $6 per day and the season extends from April until the end of November, although the hardy play all the year around. In total, there are sixteen courts: nine clay, three asphalt, and four antuga (a special mixture of crushed tile). A professional is on hand at all times to give private lessons. A complete clubhouse with pro-shop, swimming pool and restaurant is within the tennis complex.

The nearest hotel is the Stad, which is modern and air conditioned. For information regarding rates and other particulars write to the Manager, The Stad Hotel, Ankara, Turkey.

Nabil El-Khazen, the 1972 Ankara Tennis Club champion in Turkey, being congratulated by Mr. Pierre Helon, the local Minister.